S0-BCL-983

Behind Our Sunday Smiles

Helping Those with Life-Controlling Problems

Jimmy Ray Lee

BAKER BOOK HOUSE
Grand Rapids, Michigan 49516

Copyright © 1991 by
Baker Book House Company

ISBN: 0-8010-5667-5

Third printing, September 1993

Printed in the United States of America

Unless otherwise identified, Scripture quotations in this
volume are from The Holy Bible, New International Version. Copyright 1973, 1978, 1984, International Bible Society. Used by permission of Zondervan Bible Publishers.
Other Scripture quotations maked KJV are from the King
James Version of the Bible.Those identified TLB are from
The Living Bible, and those identified as PHILLIPS are
from The New Testament in Modern English, J. B. Phillips, translator.

(Persons identified as having life-controlling problems represent a composite of the author's pastoral experience
and no one individual is portrayed in this volume.)

CONTENTS

1

....

Introduction to Life-Controlling Problems

Examples and Definitions of Life-Controlling Problems

With sincere smiles on their faces, Frank and Mary (names have been changed to respect the privacy of each person mentioned) entered the Sunday morning church service. The minister marveled as he watched Frank and Mary participate in the song service and listen intently as he preached that morning. He knew that Frank and Mary were deeply concerned over Bill, their 28-year-old son whose life was controlled by alcohol and other drugs.

In their church, Joe and Debbie's marriage was looked on as a model for young couples to follow. They had two children and lived in one of the finer areas of the city. Both Joe and Debbie served in the church—Joe as a deacon and Debbie as a teacher.

After Joe completed graduate school, he entered into a solo business venture that required extensive travel. Joe spent many nights in lonely hotel rooms, watching R- and

X-rated movies geared toward sexual activities. He began the downward spiral of sexual addiction. Over a period of three to four years the addiction graduated to compulsive sexual behavior while on the road and later in his hometown. Joe was living a double lifestyle. Debbie became concerned about her husband's behavior as he became indifferent to the family and the church family. Also on several occasions she found pornographic magazines which he had left in his suitcase. Joe's life had become controlled by a sexual addiction which cost him his family, dignity, and self-esteem.

Frank and Mary's lives were affected by their son's life-controlling problem. Debbie lost her husband and her children lost their father to a life-controlling problem. A life-controlling problem is anything that masters a person's life. The apostle Paul stated his determination to overcome a life-controlling problem in 1 Corinthians 6:12: "I will not be mastered by anything."

There are a number of terms used that are descriptions of life-controlling problems including *addiction*, *dependency*, *stronghold*, *slave*, and *compulsive behavior*. Each term can be used to state that a person's life is mastered by something or someone other than God.

> Addiction exists wherever persons are internally compelled to give energy to things that are not their true desires. To define it directly, addiction is a state of compulsion, obsession, or preoccupation that enslaves a person's will and desire.[1]

The purpose of this book is to help laypeople in the local church use biblical principles to provide assistance to people at different stages of life-controlling problems. Various aspects of life-controlling problems are discussed, along with ways to help those caught in the web of such a problem. Instructions for setting up a model in the local church to organize pastoral and laity concerns for hurting people are also included.

When a person is in a state of dependency, he is in a state of being dependent and has a problem that masters him. The apostle Paul uses the word *stronghold* in 2 Corinthians 10:4 when he says there is "divine power to demolish strongholds." Charles F. Stanley describes this word as being:

> an area of sin that has become part of our lifestyle. It may be a harmful habit (drugs, fornication, smoking) or it may be an attitude (rejection, loneliness, worry, doubt). We use a whole arsenal of rationalizations and speculations to support these habits or attitudes. But the knowledge on which these strongholds are based directly opposes God's truth.[2]

The apostle Paul describes the word *slave* as a term that applies to mastery (*see* Rom 6:15–23). He also states that "sin shall not be your master" (6:14). Peter speaks of the term *slave* in relationship to mastery in 2 Peter 2:19: "for a man is a slave to whatever has mastered him."

People with a life-controlling problem are impulsive in behavior, acting without regard for the consequences of such behavior. They may eat, drink, gamble, spend, or have sexual relations on impulse. "The flip side of impulsive behavior is compulsive behavior. *The Oxford American Dictionary* defines compulsion as 'an irresistible urge.' This is different from an impulse. A compulsion is repetitive. It is also restrictive and rigid."[3]

Basic Types of Life-Controlling Problems

The word *addiction* no longer applies just to alcohol and other drugs but includes many facets of life. There are at least three types of addictions that can master a person's life: *substance*, *behavior*, and *interaction*. Substances include drugs, alcohol, cigarettes, overeating, and so forth. Behaviors include gambling, compulsive spending, shoplifting, pornography, sex, and so forth. Those who have interaction addictions are either mastered by other people or are trying to master another person (codependent).

The twelve-step program, which is commonly used for alcoholics and drug abusers, is also being utilized for other addictions such as sex disorders, gambling, buying, eating disorders, and shoplifting. The program is successful because, regardless of whether they are substance or behavioral, addictions follow a similar process.

Addictions and Idols

Idolatry leads to addiction. When we follow idols, a choice has been made to look to a substance, behavior, or relationship for solutions that can be provided only by God. We have a *felt need* to serve a supreme being; if we choose not to serve God we will choose an idol to which we will become enslaved. Jeffrey VanVonderen says:

> Anything besides God to which we turn, positive or negative, in order to find life, value, and meaning is idolatry: money, property, jewels, sex, clothes, church buildings, educational degrees, anything! Because of Christ's performance on the cross, life, value, and purpose are available to us in gift form only. Anything we do, positive or negative, to earn that which is life by our own performance is idolatrous: robbing a bank, cheating on our spouse, people-pleasing, swindling our employer, attending church, giving 10 percent, playing the organ for twenty years, anything![4]

Following idols which lead to addictions prevents us from freely serving and loving God. All kinds of substance and behavioral dependencies lead to enslavery because everyone who makes sinful choices is a candidate for slavery to sin (*see* John 8:34). Jesus states in John 8:32 that "the truth will set you free." God spoke to Moses in Exodus 20:3: "You shall have no other gods before me." Sin, when unconfessed, strains the relationship with God that could be enjoyed by the believer (*see* Prov. 28:13; Jonah 2:8).

A very controversial question arises: Is an addiction a sin or a disease? Those who believe that addictions are sin point to the acts of the sinful nature which include a substance (drunkenness) and behavioral (sexual immorality) problem in Galatians 5:19–21. Another reference to the sinfulness of addictions is 1 Corinthians 6:9–11, which shows that a definite change occurred in the lives of the Corinthian Christians: "And that is what some of you were. But you were washed, you were sanctified, you were justified in the name of the Lord Jesus Christ and by the Spirit of our God."

Those who believe that addictions (particularly alcoholism and other chemical dependencies) are a disease state that the characteristics are progressive, primary, chronic, and fatal. In the later stages the victims are incapable of helping themselves because there is a loss of control and choice. "In the 1950's the American Medical Association voted approval of the disease concept of alcohol dependence. The term *disease* means 'deviation from a state of health.'"[5]

When sin and addiction are compared they show similar characteristics. Both are self-centered versus God-centered and cause people to live in a state of deception. Sin and addiction lead people to irresponsible behavior, including the use of various defenses to cover up their ungodly actions. Sin and addiction are progressive; people get worse before they get better if there is not an intervention. Jesus healed the man at the pool of Bethesda and later saw the man at the temple. Jesus warned him about the progressiveness of sin: "See, you are well again. Stop sinning or something worse may happen to you" (John 5:14). Sin is primary in that it is the root cause of evil. Sin produces sinners as alcohol causes alcoholism. Sin is also chronic, having continuing effects if not dealt with. Finally sin is fatal with death being the end result.

Although addictions do have the characteristics of a

disease, I must stand with the authority of God's Word as it pronounces various addictions as being a part of the sinful nature (*see* 1 Cor. 6:9–11; Gal. 5:19–21). They are sinful because God has been voided as the source of one's solution to life's needs, and these choices often develop into a disease. A noted Christian psychiatrist says:

> Physiologically, of course, some people are more prone to alcoholism than others, even after one drink. And often guilt drives them to more and more drinking. But then some people also have more of a struggle with greed, lust, smoking, anger, or overeating than others. Failure to contend with all of these is still sin.[6]

Anything that becomes the center of one's life if allowed to continue, will become the master of life. If God is not the center of a person's life, that person will probably turn to a substance, behavior, or another person for focus and meaning. David describes his enemy in Psalm 52 as one:

> who did not make God his stronghold
> but trusted in his great wealth
> and grew strong by destroying others (v. 7).

The young, rich ruler described in the Gospels (*see* Matt. 19:16–29; Mark 10:17–30; Luke 18:18–30) came to Jesus asking how to receive eternal life. When Jesus told him he would have to sell everything he had, give to the poor and follow him, the young man went away sad. This rich man's stronghold was the love of money. Everybody, not only the rich, must guard against this "greater love" of the rich young man. Paul writes: "People who want to get rich fall into temptation and a trap and into many foolish and harmful desires that plunge men into ruin and destruction. For the love of money is a root of all kinds of evil. Some people, eager for money, have wandered from the faith and pierced themselves with many griefs" (1 Tim. 6:9, 10).

This stronghold, the love of money, is the root cause of most addictions that plague our society. Although alcohol is a major cause of deaths, sicknesses, broken families, and relationships, it continues to be advertised with marketing strategies, appealing even to America's high school and elementary-age children. The demand for cocaine and other substances would soon cease if there were no profits to be made. Sexual addictions are fed by an 8 billion dollar industry of pornographic materials and also through appealing television commercials and movies. Compulsive gambling is fed by state-run lotteries. I wonder how much the love of money contributes to eating disorders. Many young women starve themselves to sickness and even death because of a greedy society that promotes an unhealthy thinness as beauty through media appeal and modeling agencies.

Being the creation of God, each of us has a need to be dependent. There is a vacuum in the heart of every human since the fall of Adam and Eve that can be filled only by Christ. After our first parents disobeyed God, they immediately recognized their nakedness. Without God's covering they hid themselves "from the LORD God among the trees of the garden" (Gen. 3:8). They soon learned that they could not escape from God. The psalmist writes:

> Where can I go from your Spirit?
> Where can I flee from your presence?
> If I go up to the heavens, you are there;
> If I make my bed in the depths, you are there (139:7, 8).

It is interesting that Adam and Eve hid among the trees. They hid among the trees because of guilt. Idols, which are false gods, can also become hiding places. Isaiah writes:

> for we have made a lie our refuge
> and falsehood [or false gods] our hiding place (28:15).

In a life where Christ is not the focus, a person is likely to center attention on a substance, behavior, or another person which will eventually become a god. David recognized the need to have God as his tower of strength. David states:

> The LORD is my rock, my fortress and my deliverer;
> my God is my rock, in whom I take refuge,
> my shield and the horn of my salvation.
> He is my stronghold, my refuge and my Savior—
> from violent men you save me (2 Sam. 22:2, 3).

The disease concept of addictions should be approached with caution. Assigning addictive substances and behaviors to the disease model tends to overlook the sinful nature of mankind. Although it is popular to label every stronghold as a disease, the church must warmly care for those caught in the web of deception with ongoing support. It takes more than a pat on the back. Sinful choices develop into lifestyles that are self-centered and destructive. The fall of man put us all in need of recovery.

Potential of Life-Controlling Problems

All people have the potential of being mastered by a substance, behavior, or relationship. At least three of every twelve people in our churches have a life-controlling problem, or come from a home where there is a family member that is affected. Many people have started the downward spiral of a stronghold, but since the problem is in the early stages it may not be recognized by others as yet. Problems that master a person's life come without warning. No one ever plans to be trapped by a dependency, yet it happens all the time.

Certain people are considered high risk for a problem with dependency. Children of alcoholics are known to be at high risk because alcoholism runs in families, regardless of whether it is hereditary or caused by an environmental influence.

An obsessive-compulsive person is prone to have addictive tendencies. Patrick Carnes says in his work on understanding sexual addiction:

> Addicts often point to connection between their addiction and the stress of high performance demands where there is important personal investment. Graduate school, for example, is often when addicts first encounter compulsiveness. The stress of proving one's self in an arena where every inadequacy is evaluated is a potent flashpoint for the ignition of sexual addiction. So are new jobs, promotions, and solo business ventures. Unstructured time, a heavy responsibility for self-direction, and high demands for excellence seem to be the common elements in these situations which are easy triggers for addictive behaviors.[7]

A Biblical Example

Genesis 4 records the account of Cain and a problem that mastered his life. He and his brother, Abel, brought their offerings to the Lord. Abel's offering was accepted but Cain's fruits of the ground were not received by the Lord. Cain became very angry and his face displayed his feelings. The Lord saw his anger and facial expressions and encouraged him to do what was right, so his offering and he would be accepted.

The Lord followed with a statement which illustrates how problems can become our master. He said: "But if you do not do what is right, sin is crouching at your door; it desires to have you, but you must master it" (Gen. 4:7). The Lord recognized a potential life-controlling problem crouching and ready to pounce on Cain if he opened the door. Cain did open the door and anger became his master. He invited Abel to the field and killed him. When the Lord asked where Abel was, Cain responded, trying to cover his evil actions by denying any knowledge of his brother's whereabouts.

Allowing anger to rule his life, Cain committed murder,

became a restless wanderer, and went from the presence of the Lord, alienating himself from God. Fed by jealousy, rebellion, and unbelief, anger became a stronghold in his life. This is an example of a life-controlling problem that is permitted to continue without intervention.

Stages of Life-Controlling Problems

John was sent to the principal by the high school English teacher because she smelled alcohol on his breath. During John's discussion with the principal and his parents, he insisted that this was the first time that he had ever drunk alcohol. Actually John had been drinking alcohol and using other drugs for about two years; however, this time he was careless and was caught.

Jane's life-controlling problem resulted in the tragic death of her mother. On a Monday evening in July she accidently shot her mother during a drunken stupor. When her minister visited her in jail the next day, she was in severe emotional pain and did not want to live.

Sue's life-controlling problem developed over a period of ten years. When she was twelve she had her first beer at a weekend party at a friend's house. During her high school and college years, her chemical dependency continued to develop. She was in and out of trouble with her Christian parents, police, and school officials most of her teenage years. She eventually was sentenced to jail for burglary. Two weeks after Sue completed the jail sentence, her mother died.

People who are mastered by substance and behavioral addictions follow predictable steps. Addictions normally develop over a period of time—six months or a span of many years. A person who has become enslaved to a stronghold has probably been involved for a significant period of time; there are few exceptions (LSD, PCP, and crack are not predictable and can cause serious physical and psychological reactions with the first use). "People have frequently gone through severe emotional crises because of PCP or LSD. Alcohol, on the other hand, is more predictable in its effects."[8]

Stages and Characteristics

Most people get involved with an addiction to receive a feeling of euphoria. Alcohol or other drugs, sex, pornographic literature, gambling, and so forth, produce a temporary high or euphoria.

Vernon E. Johnson, the founder and president emeritus of the Johnson Institute in Minneapolis has observed (without trying to prove any theory) "literally thousands of alcoholics, their families, and other people surrounding them . . . we came up with the discovery that alcoholics showed certain specific conditions with a remarkable consistency."[9] Dr. Johnson uses a feeling chart to illustrate how alcoholism follows an emotional pattern. He identifies four phases: (1) learns mood swing, (2) seeks mood swing, (3) harmful dependency, (4) using to feel normal. Many of the observations that have been made by Dr. Johnson and others, including myself, can also be related to other types of dependencies, although the terminology may differ.

The first phase is experimental. During this phase the person will learn the mood swing. The substance used or the behavior practiced will make the user feel euphoric for a short time. A return to normal feelings soon follows. Greg, a salesman, learns that he can turn on a sexually

Phase 1
Experimental

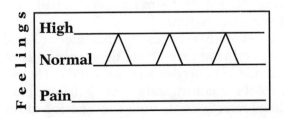

explicit R- or X-rated movie and receive a high. Marty, a young junior-high-school student learns that a beer makes him feel good. Greg, who watches the sexual movie, learns that he can trust such an experience to give him a high after having a tough day at the office or on the road. Marty learns that the beer can be trusted to make him feel good, even after a bad day at school. Although Greg and Marty are at different age levels, and one is dealing with a behavior and the other a substance, both receive feelings of euphoria from their experience. Neither of them recognizes any serious consequences. Greg and Marty begin to make plans for their practice and use and this starts the next phase toward addiction: the *social phase*. They begin to associate fun and good

Phase 2
Social

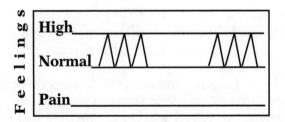

times with their behavior and substance of choice. They now seek the mood swing to feel good and usually return to normal feelings after their use or practice. Greg begins to make plans to watch X-rated movies and occasionally uses an escort service while on the road. *Playboy* and *Penthouse* join the *Wall Street Journal* as being among his favorite reading material.

In this stage Marty learns that alcohol adds to an already good time. He starts developing his own self-imposed rules, "I only drink on weekends." He has learned to control the quantity and times he drinks, but the control will be effective only for a short period of time.

Both Greg's and Marty's choice of "getting high" has become a stronghold in their lives. They are losing control of their choice of when to get high and the next stage, *harmful dependency*, is entered. Greg now becomes very compulsive in his sexual behavior. He has developed certain rituals in his life, which include cruising the college campus looking for women, visiting porn shops, and practicing compulsive masturbation. Wanting others to think he is normal, he continues to try to live a double life, but one day he will be seen entering a porn shop by a friend.

Marty begins to break his self-imposed rule of drinking only on weekends. Entering his high school years, he begins to experience loss of control and can no longer

Phase 3
Harmful Dependency

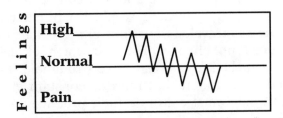

predict the outcome of his alcohol and other drug (marijuana and qualudes) use. As he uses drugs in this stage, he no longer returns to a normal feeling after the high but almost routinely experiences emotional pain.

He has changed his lifestyle and friends. His close friends are those who are using as much or more than he uses. He has developed negative feelings about himself and acts out these feelings of anger, rebellion, and antisocial behaviors. His behavior has cost him something he valued. Because he stole some of his mother's prize possessions to support his growing addiction, their relationship has been severed.

Phase 4
Using/Practicing to Feel Normal

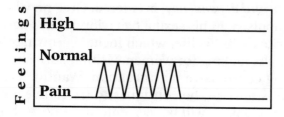

Marty's and Greg's allurements have turned into addictions without warning. The fourth stage of using or practicing to feel normal has caught up with them. Greg's continued compulsive sexual behavior has led him to a state of despair. He has tried over and over again to quit but without success. He has made promises to himself to quit by a certain day but he never fulfills his promise. Marty also is experiencing a loss of control and choice. Thinking that a new location would give him a fresh start on life, he has traveled to various cities to start over but experienced no change. The self-worth of each has become attached to his respective stronghold. Both are enslaved to the point that there is constant emotional pain and they must continue their practice and use to feel normal.

People who have a stronghold in their lives commonly go through a cycle in their downfall. Patrick Carnes in his work on understanding sexual addictions says:

> For sexual addicts an addictive experience progresses through a four-step cycle which intensifies with each repetition:
>
> 1. Preoccupation—the trance or mood wherein the addicts' minds are completely engrossed with thoughts of sex. This mental state creates an obsessive search for sexual stimulation.
> 2. Ritualization—the addicts' own special routines which lead up to the sexual behavior. The ritual

intensifies the preoccupation, adding arousal and excitement.

3. Compulsive sexual behavior—the actual sexual act, which is the end goal of the preoccupation and ritualization. Sexual addicts are unable to control or stop this behavior.

4. Despair—the feeling of utter hopelessness addicts have about their behavior and their powerlessness.[10]

Compulsive gambling is another example of a stronghold that has predictable steps. Gamblers have symptoms similar to those addicted to alcohol and other drugs. Their moods can be drastically affected and they can have withdrawal symptoms. Compulsive gambling is increasingly being seen as following the course of other addictions. "Gamblers show dependence on gambling, tolerance, meaning that they need to gamble for increasingly larger amounts of money and to gamble more frequently."[11]

Because of gambling a prominent athlete was recently barred for life from the sport in which he participated. There were testimonies indicating that he owed large amounts of money. It seems likely that he was gambling to feel normal (stage 4) as evidenced by his lack of control which was shown by his betting on his own sport.

Biblical Examples

The concept of life-controlling stages is addressed in James 1:14, 15: "but each one is tempted when, by his own evil desire, he is dragged away and enticed. Then, after desire has conceived, it gives birth to sin; and sin, when it is full-grown, gives birth to death." The downward spiral starts with *temptation* (an attraction to). The second stage is *desire* (to long for). Desire conceives and gives birth to the third stage, *sin*. The final stage is *death*.

James' concept of life-controlling problems can be compared with a marriage to an addiction. The marriage begins with *courtship*. Although initially the victim may not recognize the courtship as such because it is appealing, the victim is tempted and drawn to an addiction. The victim is enticed and allured into a relationship and gives *consent*. An addiction takes hold with a *conception* of a problem that now starts to master life.

Months or even years later there is the birth of a *child* (trouble). Including problems in the home, church, school, and workplace, the fruit of the life-controlling problem causes all kinds of problems. The relationship arrives at a place of *completion*. In this stage the marriage has become fatalistic (destructive relationship) to the victim and has hurt those that are close. The end result is *corruption*. If the relationship is not broken with the addiction, death always follows: spiritual, emotional, physical.

There are certain stages involved in David's sin with Bathsheba as recorded in 2 Samuel 11. In stage 1, "From the roof he saw a woman bathing" (v. 2). David entered stage 2 when he "sent someone to find out about her" (v. 3). In the third stage "David sent messengers to get her. She came to him, and he slept with her" (v. 4). To further complicate matters, David tried to cover up his sin which led to the murder of Bathsheba's husband.

Joshua 7 discusses Achan's sin of disobedience which led to his death. After the Lord delivered Jericho into the hands of Joshua and the Israelites, they were commanded to stay away from the sacred things which included "all the silver and gold and the articles of bronze and iron" (6:19). Achan's sin was a violation of this command and was committed in stages. In the first stage he "saw in the plunder a beautiful robe from Babylonia, two hundred shekels of silver and a wedge of gold weighing fifty shekels" (7:21). Achan followed his temptation by coveting the riches (stage 2). Then he took them (stage 3) and hid them. In addition to his own death, his sin adversely affected the entire nation of Israel, just as life-controlling problems often go beyond the victim hurting many people.

As a rule with few exceptions, life-controlling problems

do not occur overnight. I have met with parents who have tragically lost a child to chemical dependency. Many times they wanted to think that the child had just started using drugs. Also there was the wife who caught her husband entertaining a prostitute and she believed his insistence that this was the first time. Actually, for those who reach the ultimate end of their addiction, whether physical death or emotional and spiritual death, their death occurred on the *installment plan*. They died one phase at a time. Paul writes: "For the wages of sin is death, but the gift of God is eternal life in Christ Jesus our Lord" (Rom. 6:23).

Denial and Delusion

Bob's phone rang at the office one cold February day and the caller was the high school principal, Mr. Chambers. Mr. Chambers had some bad news for Bob and his wife, Carolyn. During the lunch hour, their son, Tom, had been caught smoking pot with two other members of the football team. This was particularly tough for Bob and Carolyn since they were strongly committed Christians and had raised Tom according to these values. Also, this was the second time he had been caught at school and his lifestyle and friends had changed to reflect his chemical use.

Over a period of two to three years Bob and Carolyn had noticed their son's increasing indifference and unconcern toward their family life. It seemed as though he lived in a world of his own surrounded by walls. After Mr. Chamber's call, Bob took the suggestion of a Christian counselor. He decided to make Tom responsible for his actions. Bob insisted that the principal call the police and have Tom arrested. Tom was sent to the juvenile detention center where Bob met his sixteen-year-old son. Denying he had a problem with chemicals, Tom was irate and accused his father of being a noncaring, worthless parent.

Bob and Carolyn (although she had second thoughts) felt there was no other choice but to send Tom to a treatment program hoping to help him with his dependency. A few months later Tom's parents were surprised when he thanked them for having him arrested and forced into treatment. He told them he was thankful because at the time of his arrest he was blind to what was actually happening in his life.

Aspects of Delusion

Denial and delusion are chief characteristics seen in those who are struggling with dependencies. When denial continues over a period of time, it results in delusion. J. Keith Miller in his work on deadly addictions says:

> the two characteristics of the Sin-disease. . . "denial" and "delusion," are almost universal. Denial by definition means not being able to see the ever-widening split between what one says and what one is. . . . Delusion is seeing things that are true and acting as they are *not* true. Delusion recreates reality around a person to make it less threatening to his or her self-centered (Sin) position.[12]

Delusion is sincere. A wife said to her neglectful husband, "Don't you see what your gambling is doing to the children and to me?" He replied, "It's no big deal. You're the problem, not me." Even though the family was struggling to survive because of his addiction, he sincerely believed that his gambling was not affecting them and blamed his wife. A young lady, weighing only eighty-five pounds, stares at herself in the mirror. She sees herself as being fat.

A person in delusion is a person that is misled, "a deluded heart misleads him; he cannot save himself, or say, 'Is not this thing in my right hand a lie?'" (Isa. 44:20). The apostle Paul writes in (2 Corinthians 4:4), "The god of this age has blinded the minds of unbelievers, so that they cannot see the light of the gospel of the glory of Christ." They have no sense of reality of the truth because their thinking is distorted. "He will believe his statements to himself such as, 'A little drink never hurt anyone.' 'I've been working hard, I've earned it.' 'Most women are asking to be raped.' 'I can take it or leave it.' 'I'm not really as heavy as people say I am.' 'If you had to live with my wife, you'd drink too.'"[13]

Delusion is extremely strong because it is very difficult for people to see themselves as they really are. In his work on chemical dependency Jeffrey VanVonderen states:

> Quite some time ago I heard a statistic that has remained with me and has been a great source of comfort to many families with whom I have worked. The statistic states that an average of fifty-four confrontations of his chemical problem are necessary for a dependent person to realize he has a chemical problem. You would think this would be depressing to those who are trying to help a chemically dependent person, but actually it has the potential of being very freeing and encouraging. The statistic means that there is hope, that people eventually realize their need for help. It means that one person does not carry the entire burden of helping someone realize his problem. It means that each individual step or effort is not wasted, even if it appears as such at the time.[14]

There is an old adage which is common among many people who have worked with dependent people. They say, "A person must hit bottom before he can get help"; however, a helper can *chip away* at the denial system and *raise the bottom*.

The Johari Window

This concept is an effective way to illustrate delusion. The four window panes represent a person's total self. Window pane 1 is open. The person and others recognize what is happening in this window. This open information

Johari Window

Open 1	Secret 2
Blind 3	Sub- concious 4

includes things like the weather, sports, vocation, and other interests.

Window pane 2 is secret. In this window people have secrets known only to themselves. As a trust relationship is established they may choose to reveal their secrets to others. Window pane 4 is the subconscious part and is not visible to self or others.

Window pane 3 is the blind area. These are the things that are seen by others but not recognized by the individual himself. The person with a stronghold lives mostly in window pane 3. Since such people cannot see the reality of their lives, they will need caring friends who will carefully provide feedback and pray for the Holy Spirit to open their eyes to the truth. In his work on prayer, Charles Stanley states:

> Satan pumps us full of lies which secure these strongholds. They may sound like this, "There's really nothing wrong with this music—I don't listen to the words anyway." Or, "I just drink a little when I get nervous." And haven't we all said, "The police won't pull me over for going 60 mph, so it's *ok*?"
>
> Our responsibility as Christians is to tear down these

strongholds through Spirit-filled prayers. How? There is only one weapon—the sword of the Spirit. We must fight these lies with God's Word. We must fight specific lies with specific truths.[15]

The Role of Defenses

Defenses play a major role in life of those who are in bondage to an addiction. There are behaviors people use to cover up feelings from themselves and others. After a period of time, the deluded individuals begin to believe their own excuses. Defenses are like a fortress surrounding and preventing the conquering of the stronghold, and keep the victims from seeing the truth of their bondage.

Rationalization is a common defense, used among those with a dependency. They give reasons as to why "it's not their fault because" or "everybody is doing it." Blaming is a defense used by our first parents. When the Lord God confronted Adam he said, "The woman you put here with me—she gave me some fruit from the tree, and I ate it" (Gen. 3:12). When the Lord God confronted Eve she blamed the serpent (v. 13).

After having Uriah murdered to cover up for David's sin with Bathsheba, David minimized the death of Uriah. Joab sent an account of the battle by a messenger to David stating that some men were killed along with Uriah. When David received the message he replied, "Don't let this upset you; the sword devours one as well as another" (2 Sam 11:25). By minimizing, David tried to lessen the impact of Uriah's death for which he was responsible.

Denial is a defense that prevents many people from seeing the truth. The most common form of defense is our denial that we need God. A major hurdle for all sinners is to recognize the need for Jesus Christ as Savior and Lord. The church must be on guard to this sin of denial. As the body of Christ we need each other, and when we refuse this principle God is not pleased.

The Pharisees were known for their defense of superiority. They were arrogant and self-righteous. Jesus describes their defense in Luke 18:9, "To some who were confident of their own righteousness and looked down on everybody else." Some people show their defense of superiority when they say, "I don't need to go to church," or "I can hold my liquor." "For the most part defenses, including attitudinal postures, are unintentional and automatic shields against a real or imagined threat to our self-esteem."[16] Sin goes undetected when a person is infatuated with himself. This type of superiority is recorded in Psalm 36:2:

> For in his own eyes he flatters himself
> too much to detect or hate his sin.

The Role of Feelings

David, the director of a Christian home for young men, was walking through the dormitory one morning after chapel when he noticed one of the students weeping openly. Concerned, David asked if he could assist him. Paul replied, "No, sir! I have just come to the realization that God loves me, and it is awesome!"

Paul had been in the program for two months. His feelings, not unlike others with dependencies, had been suppressed and for the first time in many years he could experience feelings again. People with life-controlling problems learn to lie about their feelings and their emotions become numb over a period of time. Vernon Johnson describes the role of feelings:

> While change is the ultimate goal, our immediate purpose is to see more accurately what needs change. This requires seeing ourselves—*discovering ourself*—and at a feeling level.
>
> In examining our purpose one of the things that stands out is our emphasis on feelings. We stress feelings for sev-

eral reasons. First of all, our behavior in the past has been so opposed to our value system that considerable feelings of remorse and self-loathing have been built up. It appears that we have accumulated a pool of negative feelings and walled them off with a variety of masks *or defenses that prevent this discovery.*[17]

Concerning the role of feelings, Paul writes in Ephesians 4:19: "Who, being past feeling, have given themselves over unto lasciviousness, to work all uncleanness with greediness"(KJV). In this passage he is encouraging the church at Ephesus not to live in delusion. They were warned not to be caught up in futile thinking, darkened understanding, and hardness of heart. These characteristics of delusion led to the numbness of feelings and the acting out of all kinds of impurities and moral uncleanness. In this passage Paul also describes the sin-disease as progressive. They had a "continual lust for more" (v. 19). Deceitful desires are associated with the old self (*see* 4:22).

The Bible provides several examples of people who express their feelings. As Jesus approached Jerusalem during the triumphal entry, he "saw the city, he wept over it" (Luke 19:41). Jesus also showed his feelings along with Mary and Martha in the death of Lazarus (*see* John 11:17–44). After Peter disowned Jesus for the third time "he went outside and wept bitterly" (Matt 26:75). In the Book of Psalms there are a number of passages in which David expresses both positive and negative feelings (*see* Pss. 32; 38; 51; 55; 56; 71; 73; 139; 143; 147). When David brought the ark of God into Jerusalem he expressed euphoric feelings by dancing before the Lord with all his might (*see* 2 Sam. 6:14). David experienced the opposite feelings when he received the news that his conspiring son Absalom was dead. The author of 2 Samuel 18:33 writes, "The king was shaken. He went up to the room over the gateway and wept. As he went, he said: "O my son Absalom! My son, my son Absalom! If only I had died instead of you—O Absalom, my son, my son!,"

David did not suppress his extreme feelings of sorrow. Although David's sin with Bathsheba caused him much pain, he effectively dealt with his feelings by expressing and taking ownership of them through a repentant heart.

Unlike the belief system of many secularists who assert that feelings are neither good nor bad, the Bible teaches otherwise. There are sinful and nonsinful feelings. Sinful feelings include jealousy, greed, and lust, whereas grief and sorrow can be described as nonsinful feelings. Both sinful and nonsinful feelings are real. But to deny them leads to their burial and a possible explosion. Keith Miller states:

> Our feelings constitute a wonderful "warning system" that tells us when we need to focus on a certain danger area in our lives or something that needs our love and attention. These feelings can activate energy and guidance to keep us safe, to heal our hurts, and to help us follow our highest ideals. But when we are in denial we bury these feelings, push them into our unconscious like pushing giant beach balls under water. . . . And when a feeling does get loose it comes up with exaggerated force "at an angle" and may hurt someone, like a beach ball that has been pushed far under water and finally pops to the surface.[18]

Not only did Jesus express his feelings while on earth, he is also concerned about our emotions. The letter written to the Hebrews emphasizes Christ's exalted position at the right hand of the Father as our high priest, however, even with his record of perfection he still identifies with our feelings. "For we have not an high priest which cannot be touched with the feeling of our infirmities; but was in all points tempted like as we are, yet without sin" (Heb. 4:15 KJV). Since he understands and sympathizes with our feelings, the writer of Hebrews encourages us to "approach the throne of grace with confidence, so that we may receive mercy and find grace to help us in our time of need" (4:16).

Without any question Jesus understands the damage that can be done when feelings are stuffed. We are urged by him to approach "the kingdom of God like a little child" (Mark 10:15). Little children are quick to trust in Jesus and they are also willing to share their feelings.

Paul writes in 1 Corinthians 14:20: "Brothers, stop thinking like children. In regard to evil be infants, but in your thinking be adults." "One does not expect a small child to understand spiritual things. . . on the other hand, children do not develop deep-seated malice or habitual faultfinding. They are quick to forgive and forget."[19] Paul recognizes the negative elements of suppressed feelings. He urges the church at Corinth to have understanding as adults, but be like children in regard to their emotions: don't stuff them. He also warns the church at Ephesus against the buildup of anger. He does not discourage anger; however, he does say in Ephesians 4:26–27, "Do not let the sun go down while you are still angry, and do not give the devil a foothold."

It is common for persons in delusion to build a wall of defenses around themselves which help them suppress and harden their feelings. There are many examples of delusion throughout the Bible. When Moses led the children of Israel out of bondage, they became blind to what God had done for them. God sent Isaiah to people who could hear but not understand and could see but not perceive.

Jesus recognized the delusion while he was on this earth. In Matthew 13:13 he describes delusion as:

"Though seeing, they do not see;
though hearing, they do not hear or understand."

Jesus recognized a degree of delusion among his own disciples. He asked them some provoking questions recorded in Mark 8:18, "Do you have eyes but fail to see, and ears but fail to hear?"

All of us have the potential of having a life-controlling

problem. Through the means of permissiveness that has slowly and persistently infiltrated our society and the church, delusion has increased. Using a human point of view versus the biblical point of view, standards and sin are being redefined in some circles. Refusing to acknowledge sin results in compounding sin. When ignored or unconfessed, sins build on each other causing delusion which can affect individuals (including the innocent), families and even nations. Isaiah warns (30:1), "Woe to the obstinate children," declares the LORD, "to those who carry out plans that are not mine, forming an alliance, but not by my Spirit, heaping sin upon sin."

The Bible is being attacked by those within and without the church. Ultimately to survive we as a nation must realize that there is no way to measure truth apart from the Bible. Our massive problems of drugs, alcohol, greediness, incest, and so forth are fed by various delusions. The writer to the Hebrews says: "For the word of God is living and active. . . it judges the thoughts and attitudes of the heart. Nothing in all creation is hidden from God's sight. Everything is uncovered and laid bare before the eyes of him to whom we must give account" (4:12, 13).

2

···

Ways to Help Hurting People

Caring and Sharing

Gene, a young, eager, and caring minister, served a church in a city of about 150,000 people. Seeking to serve Christ and the hurting people of his city, he was involved in many community activities. He worked weekly in one of the major hospitals as a chaplain, founded a Christian drug treatment program in the city, and was involved in a weekly ministry in the inner city that reached hundreds of children. He and his wife also led a convalescent ministry.

Excited to see the number of volunteers from the church and community who assisted him in the inner-city effort, Gene began to bring some of these children to the church. The Christian treatment program for boys with life-controlling problems also chose Gene's church as their home church. Every Sunday morning ten to fifteen young men, well-behaved and eager to worship God, paraded into the church and sat together on the third and fourth pews in the third section of the sanctuary.

Gene's enthusiasm was well received by his congregation at first, but lately he had begun to notice a coldness and an uneasiness developing among the congregation. Also he had heard comments from various people that concerned him. Some members said that the inner-city children should not be brought to the church but encouraged Gene and the volunteers to continue to go to them in the housing projects. Gene also noticed that the boys from the drug-rehabilitation program were not well received. They were avoided by some as if they had a terrible disease that could be transmitted by a handshake.

Saddened at what appeared to be happening, Gene tried to change the trend by preaching on the importance of reaching out to those that were hurting. Blaming himself for the lack of support from the congregation, Gene became frustrated and discouraged. The majority of the congregation did not openly object to the newcomers in the church; however, they remained neutral and unconcerned, not voicing support one way or the other. As those in the church who really wanted to reach the hurting became discouraged and one by one began to leave the church for a more accepting congregation, Gene entered a period of burnout.

In the midst of these events Gene and his wife, Brenda, befriended Roger and his wife who were wealthy but encumbered with many problems. Although Roger almost weekly was invited to attend church, he and his family probably attended Gene's local church ten to twelve times over a period of four years. Neither Roger nor his wife made any claim of knowing Jesus Christ as their Savior, but on one occasion when Gene was talking with Roger about the local Christian drug-treatment home for boys, Roger made an interesting observation. He said, "Preacher, those boys are not accepted by the people at your church. They feel they are better than those boys who are recovering from drug abuse."

Those comments by Roger stunned Gene. Yes, he knew there were many in the congregation that opposed the boys' and the inner-city children's presence in the building, but how did Roger know? His only communication with the congregation was the infrequent visits. Roger knew because of two reasons. He watched the mannerisms of the congregation during a service and saw their rejection. Second, he personally felt the same rejection toward him and his wife. It was publicly known that he had been married several times and ran an unwholesome business.

For a local church to be effective in helping the hurting, it must provide an environment for healing and growth. This involves love, acceptance, and forgiveness. Stephen V. Rexroat recalls a story about caring and sharing:

> The late Bishop Gerald Kennedy told the delightful story of a little girl who returned home late from an errand. When her mother demanded she explain her delay, the child said she had met a friend who was crying because her doll was broken. Pleased, the mother expressed surprise that her little girl had known how to fix a broken doll. But then the child said, "No, Mommy, I didn't fix her doll. I couldn't. It was broken too bad. I just sat down and helped her cry."
>
> That little girl lived a lesson we all should learn. Our call to Christian community doesn't demand we fix every broken thing. It only requires that we care. And because we care, we share in all the joys and sorrows of those we meet.[1]

An environment of caring and sharing should not be confused with giving a license to sin. Love and acceptance should be addressed in the light of firm love versus *sloppy agape*. This environment will encourage people to attend a loving church because they feel accepted. Paul describes this love and acceptance in 1 Thessalonians 2:8–12. He says: "We loved you so much that we were delighted to share with you not only the gospel of God but our lives as well. . . encouraging, comforting and urging you to live lives worthy of God, who calls you into his kingdom and glory." A loving and accepting church is one that is winning the right to be heard in the community. This New Testament church will help those who are struggling behind their Sunday smiles.

Utilizing Laypeople

A person does not need to have a Ph.D. to be a people helper. The laity can provide a valuable service in caring for the personal needs of the local church. It is impossible for the ministerial staff to deal with the hurts and staggering needs that most congregations are facing. Actually this work should be the responsibility of the local body of Christ. This is truly a significant way to release the church to ministry.

There would be more laypeople involved in helping people with life-controlling problems but they feel inadequate. Many churches have been taught that this kind of help should be limited to professionals. L. Rebecca Propst in her work on paraprofessional therapy says:

> Anthony and Carkhuff (1977) define the paraprofessional, or "functional professional" (the term they prefer), as that individual who, lacking formal credentials, performs those functions usually reserved for credentialed mental health professionals. . . various church workers would also fall in the category. . . . A review of the research in 1968 found that paraprofessionals could be trained to effect significant constructive changes in the clients they worked with.[2]

Although there is very little recent research available regarding their effectiveness, there has been an increase in the number of "functional professionals." I have observed on numerous occasions the effectiveness of laypeople in the areas of encouragement and exhortation. Their effectiveness has not always depended on their degree of education. Those who were most effective exhibited spiritual maturity, emotional stability, knew their limitations, and were blessed with Bible-based common sense.

It is true that some people are drawn to counseling-type ministries because of their own problems. Others may use the helping ministries as a way to build their own ego. "Regrettably, many who are drawn to a counseling role are insecure people intrigued by the opportunity for instant intimacy. . . others find the title 'counselor' personally fulfilling."[3] Caution should be taken to channel enthusiasm into proper directions. Paul provides solid direction in 1 Thessalonians 5:14: "And we urge you, brothers, warn those who are idle, encourage the timid, help the weak, be patient with everyone."

All of us need each other in the community of believers. We need the ministry of each other to help in the development of our walk with God and in understanding the principles of God's Word. The local church is designed to be an interdependent community accountable to the Lordship of Jesus Christ. Paul describes the church in 1 Corinthians 12:12: "The body is a unit, though it is made up of many parts; and though all its parts are many, they form one body."

Helping people with life-controlling problems should be one of the main focuses of lay ministries. It must be remembered that Jesus is the healer (*see* Acts 9:32–35). No minister or layperson can bring healing in the life of a person who is encumbered with a stronghold; however healing can occur where there is a proper environment of love and acceptance. The ultimate therapist is the Holy Spirit. A church with laypeople involved in helping ministries can be compared to a garden that has been prepared for the seed to grow. The Lord can use laypeople to clear the wound for the Great Physician to heal the brokenhearted.

Eight Core Conditions of Helping

In his adaptation of Robert Carkhuff's work, Gary Sweeten shows eight qualities that are necessary for any person to be effective in helping relationships.[4] These core conditions, when successfully used, can benefit all relationships. These qualities are a process which requires practice. Local church helpers can have great tools but without proper interpersonal skills their success will be limited. A church may choose to put big dollars into various models and programs but it will fail without proper people skills. These skills are centered on a person's tongue: "The tongue has the power of life and death. . ." (Prov. 18:21).

Accurate empathy. It is important to know the difference between empathy and sympathy. A person with accurate empathy can correctly perceive the feelings of another person without being captured by the victim's emotions. A person with sympathy actually feels what the victim feels and this may prevent him from being objective in a helping relationship since he is likely to be *caught up* in the victim's emotions.

The key to accurate empathy is understanding the pain while remaining in a neutral position. The helper's goal should be to feel *with* the hurting person versus feeling *what* the individual feels. Whenever the helper and the seeker are experiencing the same feelings of pain, the focus may become pity and prevent the healing. Compassion and understanding assist the helper in accurately perceiving the other person's feelings and experiences.

One can be effective in helping a hurting person even though he or she may not be able to identify with the problem. A popular myth is "a person must be a former drug user before he or she can help a victim of drug abuse." Jesus was effective in helping the hurting yet he was sinless.

It is true that a divorcee can relate with another

divorcee or a recovering addict can relate with a person caught in the web of an addiction. However with accurate empathy a person who has not experienced the same hurts can also be effective. The helping relationship starts with the development of trust and accurate empathy. "Two skills that appear to be easily taught to paraprofessional counselors are empathy and basic skills in cognitive behavior therapy."[5]

Warmth. Warmth is communicated primarily through nonverbal ways including eye contact, nonpossessive touch, and body language. A congregation that is warm will be accepting and caring instead of ignoring, rejecting, or giving a cold shoulder. Warmth is shown by a person's concern and affection for others.

People's inner feelings are often displayed by their tone of voice or body movement. A warm voice and a caring touch can bring peace and calmness to a brokenhearted person. Warmth communicates openness and thus lessens the defensiveness of a person seeking help and helps to build a trust relationship. Paul states in Romans 12:10 (PHILLIPS), "Let us have real warm affection for one another as between brothers, and a willingness to let the other man have the credit." Warmth is nonverbal openness which helps create an environment for healing and growth in the local church.

Respect. People with this quality display *agape* love which loves and accepts a person as he or she is. They treat other people as equals and do not put them down. Having respect for another person does not mean that the helper takes ownership of the problems or rescues from responsibilities.

This quality in a helper separates a person from behavior and looks beyond the sin and sees the person as being created by God. A genuine interest is shown in the person with the life-controlling problem. This kind of interest does not always provide quick answers but gives the person seeking help space to gain personal insight. The helper respects the topics initiated by the person seeking help and does not try to divert attention to the helper's interests. A person shows respect by understanding limitations and time restraints. There may be times when the helper must refer a person to someone else for help thus displaying respect for the individual. Every person, regardless of social or moral status, deserves respect as a human being. Peter says in 1 Peter 2:17: "Show proper respect to everyone. . . ."

Genuineness. A genuine person is not a phony and does not play the role of superiority. He or she is a truthful person, honest about feelings and does not wear a mask which presents a false image. First Thessalonians 2:5 describes Paul's genuineness: "You know we never used flattery, nor did we put on a mask to cover up greed—God is our witness." Being genuine does not mean that a person is so transparent that he or she hurts or offends people with honesty.

This quality presents a good role model. This person is consistent from day to day and is not living two lives. A genuine person does not get caught up into fads just to please others. The best example of genuineness is Jesus Christ. Paul says in Philippians 2:7 that Jesus "made himself nothing, taking the very nature of a servant, being made in human likeness." A genuine person's inner feelings are consistent with words and deeds. "Genuineness implies spontaneity without impulsiveness and honesty without cruel confrontation. It means that the helper is deeply himself or herself—not thinking or feeling one thing and saying something different."[6] A genuine person is an open individual who has nothing to prove.

Self-disclosure. A helper can share his or her own personal experiences and insight that may assist the seeker in understanding how to deal with a life-controlling problem. A helper should use caution and not overuse self-disclosure by talking too much which could shift the focus of the conversation away from the seeker.

The helper should have a clear goal for self-disclosing. Self-disclosure should not be confused with empathy which seeks to "feel with" the person. The goal is to provide insight that the person seeking help does not appear to have. While sharing with the individual, the helper should not talk down to the seeker as being inferior or as a child; rather, the person should be treated as an adult talking to another adult. Sharing insights for the purpose of helping should always be positive in conversation although the outcome may be painful. "God is not the *Author* of all events, but He is the *Master* of all events."[7] Stay at the level of insight relevant to the person's need. James says in James 5:16: "Admit your faults to one another and pray for each other so that you may be healed" (TLB). Self-disclosure should be for the purpose of bringing healing to the person enslaved by a stronghold.

Concreteness. This quality is used to help move a person from the generalities of a discussion to the specific areas of need. It is common for an individual with a life-controlling problem to provide the presenting problem before giving the real problem. The truth often comes in bits and pieces before all the facts are assembled. Gary Sweeten in his work on the eight core conditions of helping states:

> There are some basic principles which come through the Scripture in a very consistent manner. One of those principles is this: be sure to take all the facts into consideration prior to deciding a major course of action (this implies using concreteness). There are numerous proof texts to support the conclusion that concreteness is important. . . .
> There are some who believe that living by faith demands that we ignore the facts of life. However, Biblical faith enables us to look squarely at the facts and yet have faith in God's deliverance, mercy, and power.[8]

In John 6:8 Andrew presented facts to Jesus in regard to feeding the 5,000. Andrew said, "Here is a boy with five small barley loaves and two small fish, but how far will they go among so many?" (v. 9). Jesus did not ignore the facts nor did he rebuke Andrew for his lack of faith. He simply responded to the specific facts and "took the loaves, gave thanks, and distributed to those who were seated as much as they wanted. He did the same with the fish" (v. 11). Jesus acted on the facts he received from Andrew.

Confrontation. It is no accident that this quality is listed near the end of the eight core conditions of helping. There must be a display of the previous conditions such as empathy, warmth, and respect before a relationship can benefit from confrontation. Careful confrontation can be helpful in bringing about action and accountability after the helper has won the right to be heard.

The helper must be careful not to be harsh in his confrontation of a person that has a life-controlling problem. Paul says in Galatians 6:1: "Brothers, if someone is caught in a sin, you who are spiritual should restore him gently. But watch yourself, or you also may be tempted." Confrontation should not be used as a means of power or control. It should be done with sensitivity and have the purpose of helping the person break out of delusion and grow in Christ.

Immediate feedback. Focusing on the health of the relationship, this quality deals with the immediate relationship between two people. Immediate feedback cannot be effective without regular use of the other core conditions. This quality represents understanding of each other, warm acceptance, dealing with specifics, genuineness, reflection of each other's feelings, and confrontation when necessary.

Immediate feedback is necessary to prevent walls from building in a relationship. This helps individuals keep in touch with possible delusions that could develop. Paul worked hard to prevent walls from building between himself and others. In 2 Corinthians 7:8–9 he says: "Even if I caused you sorrow by my letter, I do not regret it. Though I did regret it—I see that my letter hurt you, but only for a little while—yet now I am happy, not because you were made sorry, but because your sorrow led you to repentance."

Helping or Hurting

Raymond's parents tried over and over again to help him with his drug use. At age twelve he started drinking at a friend's house on the weekend, and was dependent on alcohol and other drugs by age fifteen. He was raised by Christian parents and they attended church regularly. At age twenty-one, Raymond's life was a wreck. His drug use resulted in his killing a very close family friend, and a lengthy prison sentence.

During Raymond's teenage years, his parents contributed to his drug use, although they thought they were helping. They changed churches several times because Raymond didn't like the church, or when he was corrected by a Sunday school teacher, the parents would always side with Raymond.

Mr. Polk, the high school principal, called Raymond's mother on a Friday in the fall of the year. He had suspected for some time that Raymond was selling marijuana on the school property, but this time he knew for sure because a teacher monitoring the grounds during lunch saw him sell the substance to another student. Having received the news concerning Raymond, his mother became angry and blamed Mr. Polk and his staff for a poorly run school. She threatened to bring a lawsuit against him and the high school for bringing such an accusation against Raymond. In the conference with the principal and the teacher who caught Raymond with marijuana in his possession, the parents sided with

Raymond and gave a tongue lashing to the school officials. They transferred their son to a private, Christian
school but Raymond's behaviors and his parents' way of
dealing with his problem did not change.

During the course of one year Raymond was arrested
five times for driving under the influence of alcohol.
Each time his parents bailed him out of jail giving him
"one more chance," thinking they were helping him.
They built their life around Raymond, covering up for his
deviant behavior. The other children were neglected.
Three days before Raymond's eighteenth birthday, the
marriage of the parents ended. Their kind of "helping"
had turned into pain for the entire family.

Charles and Lois were Christian parents who had a
seventeen-year-old son addicted to chemicals. Lois called
Max, the director of a Christian drug treatment program
in their city, and asked for an appointment to discuss
their son's problem. After the parents' visit with Max, he
gave them a book to give to their son, Bill. Max agreed to
visit with their son the next day at noon. Charles and
Lois went home and gave the book to Bill, and he agreed
to meet with Max as scheduled.

The next day, a snowy day in February, Max drove up
to Bill's home. He felt the strain immediately as he
entered the home. It was apparent that the son had
drained them financially, emotionally and spiritually.
Lois greeted Max at the door and said, "Bill is in his bedroom and he doesn't want to see you." Bill was permitted
to control entry into his bedroom. Although it was
against his parents' wishes, he used drugs in his room
without their successful intervention. Permission was
needed to enter Bill's bedroom.

Observing the pain on Lois's face, Max commented, "If
it's okay with you, I will go in and see Bill anyway." It
seemed to be a relief to Lois that a person would actually
violate Bill's privacy rights. Max knocked on Bill's door
and said, "I want to talk with you, Bill." When there was
no response, Max gently opened the door and found Bill

laying on his bed, hallucinating from a chemical. Max felt uneasy but he sat down on the corner of Bill's bed and said, "Bill, what are you on?" Bill responded by handing him a folded piece of paper. Max's first thought was *Oh, it's LSD.* He opened the paper and was surprised to see a ten-dollar bill. Moving in and out of reality and euphoria, Bill, with tears in his eyes, said, "This is my last ten dollars from selling drugs at Central High School [he had dropped out four months earlier], and it's for your program." Max then noticed a written message with the money. The note said: I NEED GOD'S LOVE MORE THAN DRUGS. YET I'M CONFUSED. I FEEL USED, I WANT *off* THE MERRY-GO-ROUND OF DRUGS. Bill went into Max's program and had a remarkable recovery.

Bill's loving parents were doing what they thought was right, but permitting Bill to have privacy and use chemicals in his bedroom was hurting instead of helping. Actually Bill wanted Max to enter the bedroom without an invitation.

Enabling and Rescuing Behaviors

There is a word that is used to describe the actions of people such as the parents of Raymond and Bill. The word is *enabling.* Although there are many good uses of this word, in our context it is a negative term. Enabling is anything that stands in the way of or softens the natural consequences of a person's behavior. Although they were loving parents, they stood in the way of the consequences of their children's behaviors. Raymond's parents continually rescued him from the consequences of his deviant behavior. Charles and Lois permitted Bill to use drugs in their home, and this was a case of harming a person that they loved very much.

Unknowingly, an enabler helps the one he cares for to continue his downward spiral of addiction. He continues to help even though his assistance is being abused. Another term used for enabling is rescuing. The writer of Proverbs writes:

"A hot-tempered man must pay the penalty;
   if you rescue him, you will have to do it again" (19:19).

Helpers learn to rescue their friend or loved one from
responsibilities. "As counselor Scott Egleston says, we
rescue anytime we take responsibility for another human
being—for that person's thoughts, feelings, decisions,
behaviors, growth, well-being, problems, or destiny."[9]

Robert and Gayle were concerned about their son Eric.
Being leaders in their church, they were dismayed that
their son would even consider drinking since he had been
raised in the church. However, Eric had gotten involved
with friends at school who were a bad influence. Robert
began to find beer cans in his son's car and noticed a
change in Eric's attitude.

As hurting parents they visited with Joseph, a Christian
counselor. Joseph encouraged them to maintain their
house rules which meant that Eric was required to obey
curfew and not drink alcohol in their home.

After meeting with Joseph they had a talk with Eric,
sharing with him that they loved him very much, but he
would be expected to follow their house rules. Eric made
the decision to leave home rather than follow their rules.
As he stayed away for months, Robert and Gayle pondered their decision, wondering if he would be gone forever. Trusting God to bring him back, they prayed for his
safety.

On a Sunday night several months after Eric made the
decision to leave home Robert and Gayle, returning
home from church, were pleasantly surprised to see that
Eric had come back. He was in bed and left a personal
letter for his parents. In the letter Eric said:

   I know I'm the last person on this earth that should ask
   you for help after all you've done for me, but I really need
   help from ya'll right now. I know it seems strange writing
   you a letter, but I really don't know if I know how to talk
   to you this serious face-to-face. I guess the bottom line is

I'm hooked on drugs and alcohol and need help (counseling?) to straighten myself up before it's too late. . . . I'd be so thankful. Any extra expenses that come out of this ordeal are fully understood to be taken care of by me and the sooner the better. If I can't change my ways now, I know I can never amount to anything. I love you very much and don't ever want to hurt you or myself anymore.

Love, your son,
ERIC

Robert called Joseph and set up an appointment for Eric, himself, and his wife. Eric was serious in his commitment to change and entered into a Christian rehabilitation program that dealt with life-controlling problems. His life was changed, and his family was reunited.

Although they loved him very much, Robert and Gayle did not enable Eric. They did not loosen the standards of their home nor did they try to rescue Eric after he made the decision to leave home. This was difficult for them as loving parents because they knew he had a trail of problems following him.

Biblical Examples

First Kings 21 records the enabling behaviors of Jezebel. Her husband, King Ahab, became angry and pouted because Naboth would not sell him his vineyard. When Jezebel noticed Ahab and his sullen condition, she devised a deceitful plan that would get the vineyard for him and rescue him from his pouting spell.

Using the official seal, she wrote letters in her husband's name, declaring a day of fasting. She placed Naboth in a prominent position and had two scoundrels testify against him saying that he was guilty of cursing God and King Ahab. Jezebel's enabling behavior led to the death of Naboth. The writer of 1 Kings describes Jezebel as a person who urged Ahab to do evil (*see* 21:25).

The prodigal son chose to take his part of the inheritance and leave home (see Luke 15:11–32). He went to a distant country and wasted his wealth. Having run out of money, he worked in a citizen's field, feeding pigs. He finally came to his senses, or broke out of his delusion, and said: "I will set out and go back to my father and say to him: Father, I have sinned against heaven and against you" (v. 18). His father welcomed him home with acceptance and compassionate love.

The father exhibits characteristics of a person who helps instead of hurts. Although it was painful to see his son leave, the father did not attempt to rescue his son from the decision he made. Luke writes in verse 16: ". . . but no one gave him anything." The father helped his son break out of delusion by not enabling him. The son recognized his sin, confessed it, and received mercy from his father. Being a good father, he was certainly praying for his son, watching for his return, and waiting to receive him with open arms. The prodigal son's father was not an enabler; he allowed his son to be responsible for his own actions.

There is a biblical principle that deals with the enabling behaviors. Paul writes: "Do not be deceived; God cannot be mocked. A man reaps what he sows" (Gal. 6:7). "Praying that God will keep the person from getting into trouble is not helpful. Pray, instead, that God will bring as much trouble into the person's life as it will take to convince him that his life is failing and he is needy."[10] People, as well-intentioned helpers, may hinder God by their enabling behaviors. Behind their Sunday smiles, many Christians come to church with a heavy heart for a friend or loved one enslaved by a stronghold, but their enabling behaviors may be hindering rather than helping that person's recovery.

Family Emotional Stages

Elisabeth Kübler-Ross describes a five-step process that dying people experience in accepting their death. The five steps are *denial, anger, bargaining, depression,* and *acceptance*.[11] A family who has one of its members affected by a life-controlling problem will experience the same process.

According to mental health professionals, people experience these stages whenever there is any loss, major or minor. They may go through the stages as listed or they may jump back and forth from one to another. Although he was physically alive, the prodigal son's father recognized his son as being dead. Luke writes (15:24), "For this son of mine was dead and is alive again."

Denial

Sue was surprised when she received a call from the police telling her that her daughter had been arrested at the shopping mall for shoplifting. She denied that Jennifer could do this because she had everything a sixteen-year-old girl could want. The family lived in the nicest area in the city. They had a swimming pool in their backyard, membership to the country club, and Jennifer had her own sports car.

Sue refused to accept the reality that Jennifer was a shoplifter. She said, "There must be a mistake; Jennifer would not do such a thing. Besides, taking a ten-dollar bracelet, is no big deal! After all, girls go through these stages when they sow their wild oats." Sue felt that she was in control of Jennifer and could shield her from future problems. She used denial to help herself with the shock and for protection from reality.

To help a person in denial, the helper should work to gain the denier's confidence. The person suffering from denial needs help in feeling safe to the point of taking a look at what is really happening. The helper needs to see that the victim is controlling his or her life and denial distorts thinking.

Anger

While sitting at her office completing a business deal with a client on Tuesday afternoon, Sue received a call

from the high school principal. He asked her to come to
the school immediately because Jennifer had stolen a wal-
let from one of the students. Sue became angry and
cursed him on the telephone. She told the principal that
the environment at the school contributed to drugs and
stealing.

After thinking more about Jennifer, Sue became angry
with God and herself. She blamed God for the problem.
She angrily talked to God saying, "Why me, God? Why is
this happening? Jennifer has everything that a teenager
could want."

Sue blamed herself. She said, "If I were a better person, Jennifer would not be getting into trouble." She
blamed the church youth program for not "having a good
enough ministry to help Jennifer stay out of trouble."

It was common for Sue and Jennifer to get into physical fights. Sue called their minister and his wife to come
to their house one evening after a fight, and they noticed
that Sue was bruised and scratched and the banister to
the stairway was broken from the altercation. Sue was in
emotional pain and her crying would not stop. After the
fight, Jennifer got into her car and left in an emotional
rage. Sue was concerned for Jennifer's safety and asked
her minister for help.

A person in the anger stage needs help in seeing how
his or her life is being controlled and preoccupied by the
victim. Being aware of the anger and not permitting it to
become a stronghold is important (*see* Eph. 4:26, 27). A
person in the angry stage should be encouraged to share
feelings. Helping the person to take a look at what the
anger is doing to the marital relationship is also encouraged. The helper needs to be a good listener, remembering that the anger stage is normal.

Bargaining

Sue began to strike a bargain with herself, others, and
God. She contracted with herself to be a better house-

keeper and to lose twenty pounds within sixty days. She also struck a deal with Jennifer. She agreed to buy her a new car if she would refrain from shoplifting.

Deals were made with God in behalf of Jennifer. Sue promised to join the PTA if God would help Jennifer stop shoplifting. She also promised to teach a Sunday school class and increase her financial support of the church.

A person in this stage needs to understand that help for a friend or loved one does not depend on one's performance. None of us is good enough to merit God's help. Paul writes in Romans 3:23, 24): "for all have sinned and fall short of the glory of God, and are justified freely by his grace through the redemption that came by Jesus Christ." The helper should encourage the bargainer to look closely at our powerlessness to change another person.

Depression

In this stage Sue began to experience extensive pain because she saw no hope for Jennifer. With reality setting in, she felt the pain of losing a child to shoplifting. Grief filled her life when she thought about her parental relationship to Jennifer. This time was particularly tough for Sue because she felt the pain of a marriage to a passive husband and father to Jennifer.

Melody Beattie in her work on the grief process states:

> When we see our bargain has not worked, when we finally become exhausted from our struggle to ward off reality, and when we decide to acknowledge what life has socked to us we become sad, sometimes terribly depressed. This is the essence of grief: mourning at its fullest. This is what we have been attempting at all costs to avoid. This is the time to cry, and it hurts. This stage of the process begins when we humbly surrender, says Esther Olson, a family counselor who works with the grief, or as she calls it, "forgiveness process." It will disappear, she says, only when the process has been worked out and through.[12]

Depression is generally brought on by the loss of something or someone. Reacting to a loss is normal in the grief process. Archibald Hart states:

> When a normal depression doesn't remit within a reasonable period of time (at the longest two weeks) then it becomes a clinical depression and should be treated . . . it is possible for a psychologically triggered depression to be just as painful and serious in its symptoms as any biologically based depression.[13]

A person in this stage needs hope and help in understanding his feelings. The helper should encourage the depressed person to share emotions. David repeatedly reports his experience with grief in the Book of Psalms. The sharing of painful emotions helps one work through the depression stage. Paul writes: "Praise be to the God and Father of our Lord Jesus Christ, the Father of compassion and the God of all comfort, who comforts us in all our troubles, so that we can comfort those in any trouble with the comfort we ourselves have received from God" (2 Cor. 1:3, 4).

Acceptance

Sue set an appointment to see her minister on a Tuesday morning. She explained to him that Jennifer was also drinking alcohol and had stolen two thousand dollars from Sue's checking account. She said, "I've had all I can take. I have given her back to God." At the suggestion of the minister, Jennifer eventually agreed to enter a Christian treatment program where she received help for her deviant behavior.

At the acceptance stage a person feels free to turn a friend or loved one over to God. This does not mean that the person condones or takes pleasure in what is happening in the victim's life; instead, the reality of the situation has been accepted. This is a time when the wounded emotionally detach themselves from the one they love so much. If the victim gets help, the persons in the acceptance stage do not feel they have to receive the credit. They have accepted their powerlessness to change another person. Paul writes in Romans 7:18: "I know that nothing good lives in me, that is, in my sinful nature. For I have the desire to do what is good, but I cannot carry it out."

The mother of Moses recognized her powerlessness to spare him from Pharaoh's decree which called for each baby boy to be thrown into the Nile River. When she could no longer hide the baby, she prepared a basket and placed him in it among the reeds on the river bank. As the sister of Moses watched, Pharaoh's daughter found the baby, spared the child, and helped him grow into adulthood. Moses became a great deliverer because his mother was willing to turn him over to God.

It is extremely important for a helping person to understand the grief process. Without this understanding a helper may give up when a person denies he or she has a problem. It may appear that the victim does not want your help or is just indifferent. If you as a helping person understand the grief process, you are not likely to take the victim's anger personally and bow out of the helping relationship.

Family Systems and Life-Controlling Problems

Judy was very excited about being asked out to the prom by her boyfriend. Since this was a special evening she asked her mom for permission to stay out beyond her scheduled curfew. Her mother, Polly, did not have a good reason to deny the request, but she felt in her heart that she should say no. She explained to Judy that she didn't have a specific reason as to why the curfew should not be extended but she had a *gut feeling* that the curfew should be honored. Judy was supposed to leave the prom no later than 12 A.M.

Very upset with her mother, Judy went to her dad,

Steve, seeking an intervention into Mom's decision. Steve
and Polly stood together in their decision, even though
Judy persisted in her request. Finally, on the day of the
prom, Polly in Steve's presence said to Judy, "Darling, we
love you very much and we trust you, however, we do not
feel good about changing the curfew."

Throughout the evening after Judy left for the prom,
Steve and Polly pondered their decision and hoped that
Judy would respect the curfew, even though she was
upset. Steve and Polly were delighted to hear the door
open at the specified time. Judy had obeyed her parents
and honored the curfew.

Later that morning, as Judy was asleep in her bed, four
teenagers were killed in a car accident. The same car
Judy would have been riding in had she chosen to break
the curfew skidded off the rain-slick road, went down an
embankment, and hit a tree. The teenagers in the car
were killed and not found until some time later in the
morning. Thinking that Judy was in the wreck, Steve's
and Polly's neighbors were terribly shaken. When Judy
and her parents returned home from church on this
Sunday morning, some of the neighbors began to weep
for joy when they saw her, and thanked God that she was
not in the accident.

Judy was fortunate to be in a Christian family that had
a solid family system. A family system is the attitudes
and patterns by which a family operates over a period of
three generations, and is characterized by each family
member being a part of the whole. In observing one's
family system, a person should picture himself or herself
as one part of the whole family unit.

When a family member has a life-controlling problem,
others in the family will operate normally within their
family system experience to resolve the problem. I have
observed three specific systems in working with families:
dysfunctional, disengaged, functional (although there is
more than one type of each).

The Dysfunctional Family

Dysfunctional families are a tragic and growing part of the North American landscape. This specific type of family is the one in which the authority line between the parents and children is blurry. In this family it is hard to detect who is in charge. Teenagers make decisions in regard to their well-being that should be made by their parents. Sixteen-year-old Mike was permitted to drink alcohol because his parents thought he needed his space to make his own decisions. He was involved with other teenagers who were a bad influence, but the parents would not interfere with Mike's decision.

In this type of family the parents live for and compete for the children. They learn to live their lives through their children. Some fathers may press their sons to excel in sports because they were never successful themselves. Having an unfulfilled desire to march in front of the high school or college band, some mothers may push their daughters to be outstanding majorettes. The parents blame each other for problems they encounter. They put on a good front for others and maintain a supply of defenses to cover up their behaviors.

It is common for coalitions to develop with one of the parents working as an enabler to the child with deviant behavior. The other parent may have close ties to the child that is *straight*. If there are other children, they may not be a part of either coalition. The emotions between the parents are broken down, and they may relate to the children better than to each other.

In an attempt to maintain family stability, some parents may use another person or object to prevent the son or daughter with a life-controlling problem from exploding the family relationship. Triangles are common in dysfunctional families. A parent may sit with a *problem child* in a room where the television set is the third leg of the triangle. Their focus will be on the television program instead of dealing with the problem. Parents may focus on the son or daughter with a life-controlling problem in a triangle relationship to avoid issues among themselves. Triangles serve to break down communications and prolong the agony of a dysfunctional family.

The Disengaged Family

In this type of family there is a very strong authority line between the parents and children with very little going on emotionally. The boundaries in this family are rigid with a lack of communications. This family unit is characterized by one of the parents being legalistic or unyielding and the other parent being passive. The teenagers in this family normally go their own way.

Mary was dismayed when she found that her son was heavily involved in drugs. She was encouraged by a Christian friend to visit with a counselor. In her conversation with the counselor she timidly discussed her son, but with the understanding that the counselor would not tell her husband of the visit. She said, "If my husband learns of Joe's problem with drugs, he will hurt him." In this situation the counselor urged a meeting with both parents to reach a better understanding. He knew that in this type of family it often takes a family member's problem reaching a crisis point before the family responds.

The Functional Family

Communication lines are open between the parents and children in this type of family system. Children have input into family matters; however, the parents make the final decision in regard to the child's well-being. Steve and Polly listened to Judy's request for an extension of the curfew on prom night, but they felt it was in the best interest of Judy for them not to extend the curfew.

This family unit is characterized by a sense of family wholeness. Each family member has a feeling of belonging which contributes to their personal self-esteem. This is an open system where friends can be invited into the home without the family feeling they must protect themselves.

The characteristics of a functional family are described by Paul in Ephesians 5:21–6:4. Each family member has a role to play in God's plan for the family. This unit functions properly when there is submission to Christ. Husband and wife are admonished to stand together as one in Christ. Paul writes in verse 31: "For this reason a man will leave his father and mother and be united to his wife, and the two will become one flesh." Even though Judy tried to convince her father that he should side with her and permit the curfew extension, Steve stood with Polly in her decision.

Paul describes checks and balances to prevent abuse and neglect in the family unit. The entire unit operates under the lordship of Jesus Christ. The functional family parents are male and female, not two of the same sex cohabitating together. Wives are to submit to their husbands but husbands are admonished to love their wives. Paul writes in verse 25: "Husbands, love your wives, just as Christ loved the church and gave himself up for her." This is a strong check for husbands with no room for abuse or neglect of the wife.

Children are to grow under the *godly covering* of their parents. Paul writes in Ephesians 6:1, 2: "Children, obey your parents in the Lord, for this is right. Honor your father and mother—which is the first commandment with a promise." Even though she disliked it, Judy honored her parents' decision, recognizing their authority (*godly covering*).

Children need to see a loving relationship between their parents. Spouses who love and respect each other contribute greatly to the children's sense of well-being. Children face far less emotional problems when parents are affectionate toward one another. It helps prepare the children emotionally for personal relationships and marriage. Parents who openly express their appreciation for each other enhance their children's sense of security.

Much attention has been given to children in this country. This has caused us to become a child-centered society. Certainly children need our attention, however parents must guard against the love of the family being focused solely on the children. Such a focus can cause the disintegration of the marriage over a period of time. When children become the center of family love, the love affair between the mom and dad may grow cold. When the children grow up and leave home, the parents may face difficulty in staying together because the flame has disappeared.

Children Rebel

Children should be taught that they are accountable to God for their actions as are parents responsible to be a godly covering for them. Solomon writes in Proverbs 1:8: "Listen, my son, to your father's instruction and do not forsake your mother's teaching." Children should be made aware of God's law of authority, even though we live in a society that is unbalanced in its declaration of rights and responsibilities. Much emphasis is placed on personal rights but very little is said about being responsible for our own actions. Paul writes in Romans 13:1: "Everyone must submit himself to governing authorities, for there is no authority except that which God has established."

If children refuse to walk under their parental covering (authority), they should be taught that there will always be another authority in line. However, the next first line of authority under God may not be as kind and caring as their parents. For example, if Johnny refuses to obey his godly (parental) covering and decides to use drugs, his authority may become a judge, prison, or hospital system.

Having a functional family system does not guarantee that children will never go astray. Children have choices to make also, and it is not right to always pin the blame on parents. Youth are instructed in Proverbs 4 to guard their hearts against the wicked. If children rebel, parents should keep the communication lines open but hold their loved one accountable for his or her actions.

Paul warns fathers against the abuse and neglect of the children. He writes in Ephesians 6:4: "Fathers, do not exasperate your children; instead, bring them up in the training and instruction of the Lord." The functional family is characterized by loving parents who serve as role models. Moses writes:

> "Only be careful, and watch yourselves closely so that you do not forget the things your eyes have seen or let them slip from your heart as long as you live. Teach them to your children and to the children after them" (Deut. 4:9).

With the decline in role models in various walks of life, including sports, religion, and politics, children desperately need to have parents who are good role models. "Don't do as I do, do as I say" is poor logic. Children will learn to pattern their behaviors based on what they see from their parents. Children in functional families will learn more from the values that are modeled by their parents versus those taught but not practiced.

Boundaries for children are established by the parents in the functional family. Jude writes: "Stay always within the boundaries where God's love can reach and bless you" (Jude 21 TLB). Young people will have more respect for rules established if there are open communications between the parents and children. If the boundaries are broken, then the youth should be held accountable for their actions.

Young people want boundaries. As they become older, young people will resent their parents not providing these boundaries. These boundaries help to provide a "safety zone" for the children. Sometimes the boundaries give them a good reason to say no when they may otherwise give in to negative peer pressure. I heard a seventeen-year-old high school student say, "I wish my father would ask me not to drink." After receiving help another student, who was chemically dependent, thanked his parents for intervening in his addiction.

In the functional family, parents will know where their teenagers are and with whom they associate. They will find out the answers to such questions as "Is alcohol served in the home where the teenager has been invited to attend a party?" "Will there be adult supervision?" "What time does the party end?" The parents will have a curfew and insist on its observance.

Children need help in dealing with negative peer pressure. Paul writes: "Do not be misled: 'Bad company corrupts good character'" (1 Cor. 15:33). Peer pressure not only affects young people, it can also influence parents. They may try to "keep up with the Joneses" or spend too much time with their peers and not enough quality time with their teenagers. The lack of attention from parents can cause children to turn to their own friends for their values, acceptance, and self-esteem. In the functional family the parents are the first line of defense for the children against negative peer pressure. Recognizing the need for open communication with their children, the parents do not expect the local church youth group or high school to take on this primary responsibility. An effective church youth group can be tremendous support for teens during their formative years but it does not take the place of parents in a functional system.

Single-parent homes are not necessarily dysfunctional. The authority lines already described in the dysfunctional, disengaged, and functional systems are the same except there is only one parent instead of two. The single-parent home can be functional when the communication lines are open with the children. As in two-parent homes, the single parent is encouraged to make the final decision in regard to children's well-being. Sometimes the single parent is helped in a desire for a functional family by children who notice a mom's or dad's hard work in caring for the family. The local church can be the extended family for the single-parent home.

Helpers working with families affected by a member's life-controlling problem should encourage parents to stand together guarding against coalitions. When a single parent makes a decision to stand firm, or a husband and wife stand together in helping their son or daughter, it is not uncommon for the child to try to start a coalition with a grandparent or a friend close to the family.

The helper should remember that each person is not an island. Each person is a part of a family system. Although dysfunctional patterns may have developed over a period of years, helpers can encourage family members to restore proper relationships.

Communicating with People in Delusion

People who are enslaved to a stronghold are difficult to communicate with because denial has led them to blindness of their condition. Jim Holwerda and David Egner in their work on addiction state:

> The fantasy world of an addict is more important to him than the real world. As he lets his thoughts go, he becomes convinced that the scenario he constructs to support his addiction is true. When shoplifters are caught, for example, they are often startled. The reality of the truth that they were stealing had been distorted. They had not realistically considered that they might face arrest or jail or embarrassment—the real consequences of their behavior. . . .
>
> Along with distortion is a breakdown in logical thinking. The addicted person, for example, refuses to link alcohol abuse with impaired driving. Or sexual sin with a threat to his marriage. Or compulsive spending with bankruptcy.
>
> The Lord was crystal-clear in the Scriptures in setting forth the principle of sowing and reaping. But the addicted person won't accept it because he isn't thinking straight. He may often say when caught, "I can't believe it was me doing this. . . ."
>
> The addicted person actually begins to believe the lies he tells himself to justify his habit.[14]

Communication with those who have life-controlling problems is extremely important because with each communication there is a chipping away of the person's denial system. Communication is more effective when it lessens the defensive mechanisms of the person with a stronghold yet communicates the truth in a caring way.

Careful Confrontation

After concluding his sermon on Wednesday evening, Max was greeted by Martha. With tears in her eyes she requested a visit for her and her husband, Ed, to discuss their son, Gary. He was home from college for the summer and his behaviors were causing these Christian parents much pain.

On the following day Ed and Martha revealed to Max that Gary's grades had plunged near the failing level. The university was about to remove his athletic scholarship for many rule infractions, and the clincher was when he came home intoxicated last Friday evening. Gary was considered a leader in his church youth group, and had been a top-notch student in high school, respected by his peers and coaches, so these events in Gary's life over the past year concerned his parents.

An appointment was made for Gary to talk with Max. Although Gary honored the appointment, he did so with a great deal of indifference toward Max. Over a period of nine sessions, Max and Gary met together with Max care-fronting Gary concerning the downward spiral of his life which appeared to be an addiction developing. Max used the care-fronting principles by David Augsburger which include focusing feedback on: the action, not the actor; your observations, not on your conclusions; descriptions, not on judgments; ideas, information and alternatives, not advice and answers; what and how, not why.[15]

Feedback on action, not actor. Max complimented Gary as a person but focused his discussion on his behaviors.

He did this to give Gary the freedom to change without feeling personal rejection. Max was careful not to criticize Gary as a person; instead he focused on his coming home intoxicated, poor grades, and discipline infractions which were threatening his football scholarship. When Gary tried to attack Max with a war of words, Max always brought the discussion back to the facts of Gary's behavior.

It is important to focus on the person's behavior versus him as a person. Emphasis should be placed on what he *does* rather than attacking him personally.

Feedback on observations, not conclusions. Max focused on statements of facts instead of what he thought or imagined. Max noticed that Gary would not look at him, was not giving him his full attention, and seemed anxious for the discussion to conclude. Observing these actions, Max brought them to Gary's attention. A conclusion that Gary was a drunk without respect for his parents was never suggested.

Focusing on what the helper has actually seen or heard from the other person can serve as a guard against interpretation of behaviors. When a helper interprets the behavior of the one seeking help, the helper may be seen as one who jumps to conclusions.

Feedback on descriptions, not judgments. Max never judged Gary's behaviors as being good or bad. Communication lines remained open with twenty-year-old Gary because Max never placed a value judgment on his behaviors. Communications were directed toward the descriptions of Gary's behaviors in neutral language. Max described in detail each of the behaviors that Gary confessed over a period of nine weeks, therefore helping him see the clear facts of the downward spiral of his life.

By giving descriptions the helper is likely to be seen more in a neutral role, reporting on what has been seen rather than on the behavior as right or wrong.

Feedback on ideas, information and alternatives, not on advice and answers. During the last three meetings, Max began to focus with Gary on the various options open to him. Continuing to drink alcohol was an option that Gary could select. Max explained the steps of the addiction process, and Gary noted that he was in the later part of stage three. Although he told his parents that he had been intoxicated only two times in college, Gary disclosed to Max that he was drunk in excess of thirty times during the school year.

Max was careful not to use scare tactics, give pat answers, or even specifically advise Gary what to do. When Gary finally asked Max for help, Max directed him first to the Lord to mend this relationship. Next he provided Gary with positive options from which he could choose. These options included continued meetings with him, a meeting with his parents in Max's presence, attending a college in his hometown, and entering a support group at church.

When the helper is providing ideas, information, and alternatives, the receiver of help is free to select options. When the helper gives advice and answers, the one seeking help may not accept personal responsibilities. It may restrain the freedom of the receiver of help to chart a personal course of action because of dependence on the advice of another person. The seeker may also resent the helper who insists on giving advice and answers.

Feedback on what and how, not on why. Max was careful not to ask Gary why he was intoxicated over thirty times during the school year or why he would disgrace his Christian parents with such deviant behaviors. Max knew using the word *why* would only serve to raise Gary's defenses and make it more difficult to penetrate his state of delusion. Open-ended sentences using *what* and *how* were used in Max's communications with him so Gary would not feel his motives or values were being critiqued.

Observable behaviors can be described by words such

as *what, how, when* and *where. Why* may break the communications because it may serve to raise the other person's defenses by questioning his motives. Although his motives may be wrong, his delusion can be penetrated best by observed facts presented in a nonthreatening way through a helper that is depending on the Holy Spirit's guidance.

Care-fronting is a way to help communicate the truth in love thus creating an environment for healing and growth. Paul writes in Ephesians 4:15: "Speaking the truth in love, we will in all things grow up into him who is the Head, that is, Christ." Helpers should avoid trying to convict a person with a life-controlling problem to produce changed behavior. Conviction is a work of the Holy Spirit. In regard to the Holy Spirit, Jesus says in John 16:8: "When he comes, he will convict the world of guilt in regard to sin and righteousness and judgment."

John 8 records the account of the woman caught in the act of adultery. The scribes and Pharisees tried to use the law of Moses to trap Jesus by insisting that she be stoned to death. Jesus responded to them by saying "If any one of you is without sin, let him be the first to throw a stone at her" (v. 7). Her accusers then left one by one. After they left, Jesus care-fronted the lady. He said, "Then neither do I condemn you" [caring] ". . .Go now and leave your life of sin" [confronting] (v. 11).

The person enslaved by a stronghold is already under condemnation. The victim needs freedom in Christ, not further condemnation. John writes in 3:17: "For God did not send his Son into the world to condemn the world, but to save the world through him." David Augsburger in his work on careful confrontation states:

> Truth and love are the two necessary ingredients for any relationship with integrity. Love—because all positive relationships begin with friendship, appreciation, respect. And truth—because no relationship of trust can long grow from dishonesty, deceit, betrayal; it springs up from the solid stuff of integrity.

"Confrontation plus caring brings growth just as judgment plus grace brings salvation," says Howard Clinebell, Jr., a well-known pastoral counselor. . . .

Judgment cuts, even kills. If God dealt with us only in judgment, who could stand? If God reached out to us only in love, it would be a cheap grace without integrity. Mere divine permissiveness. "Anything goes" as far as heaven is concerned. Not so![16]

Care-fronters and the convicting work of the Holy Spirit go hand-in-hand in freeing a person from a life-controlling problem.

I-Messages versus You-Messages

You-messages tend to increase conflict by enhancing the other person's defense mechanism. These messages may cause the other person to feel put down, rejected, resistant, or unimportant. Examples of you-messages include: "You just don't care"; "You are a problem"; "Can't you. . . ?"; "You are so. . . ."; These types of messages hinder communication with addicted persons because they may feel attacked, labeled, or worthless.

I-messages are more effective than You-messages. I-messages tell what a person feels or how the other person's behavior is affecting him or her. This type of message helps to communicate feelings regarding the other person's behavior and the effect of it without strengthening the defenses of the other person.

I-messages deal with facts versus evaluation. They help to communicate honesty and openness. I-messages are less likely to cause harm to the relationship because the self-esteem of the other person is not attacked. An I-message is different from a you-message in that the speaker takes the responsibility for personal feelings. Examples of I-messages include: "I feel very angry because. . . ."; "I feel rejected"; "I feel hurt." Paul writes in Colossians 4:6: "Let your conversation be always full of grace, seasoned with salt, so that you may know how to answer everyone." I-messages are tools to be used when the other person has strong feelings or a life-controlling problem. It is important to use nonjudgmental messages when dealing with people who are in delusion.

Active Listening

Active listening is perhaps the most important communication tool in helping people. It demonstrates that the helper is a caring person. It shows that the helper accepts and respects the other person. Empathetic understanding is shown by the helper.

Restating what the other person said conveys that he or she is being heard and that the helper is listening. Being a mirror, reflecting back to the person with a dependency, clarifies distorted thinking. Summarizing pulls together the other person's message and draws it to a concluding point, based on what the helper has seen and heard in the conversation.

Active listening is effective in building new relationships. The helper can better understand what the person is saying by being a good listener. This helps to build the trust level and assists the person who is experiencing numb feelings to get in touch with personal emotions. Communication by active listening is a way to build up persons with a life-controlling problem by showing them that they are accepted. Paul writes in 2 Corinthians 10:8: "For even if I boast somewhat freely about the authority the Lord gave us for building you up rather than pulling you down, I will not be ashamed of it."

Active listening is not effective when the person with a stronghold is out of control (intoxicated, severely depressed) since immediate action may be needed. Biblical values and rules should never be betrayed in favor of active listening.

Effective listening is giving full attention to the person seeking help. It involves an active reception of the person's message without being passive. A helper may need to wait during periods of silence or even tears to get to the real pains the person is experiencing. Eye contact with appropriate receptive gestures will help the person know that the helper is giving full attention. James writes in 1:19: ". . . Everyone should be quick to listen, slow to speak and slow to become angry."

Benefits of Leveling

As Max met with Gary over the nine-week period concerning his alcohol use while away in college, Gary gradually leveled with him. At first he would not admit to having a problem: however, Max continued to listen actively to Gary using care-fronting principles. Max penetrated his delusion using *I-messages* which did not raise Gary's defenses. Layer-by-layer and step-by-step Max carefully led Gary to the realization that he had a serious problem with alcohol. Seeing his powerlessness to overcome his problem without the Lord and caring friends, Gary began to level.

Leveling is the key to breaking out of delusion. The helper should assist the person with a dependency in leveling with God, self, and others. Luke provides the account of the tax collector leveling with God. Luke writes in 18:13: "But the tax collector stood at a distance. He would not even look up to heaven, but beat his breast and said, 'God, have mercy on me, a sinner.'" Because the tax collector leveled, God granted this man justification. The opposite of leveling is covering up or using defenses to protect oneself from the truth. John writes: "If we confess our sins, he is faithful and just and will forgive us our sins and purify us from all unrighteousness" (1 John 1:9).

When a person enslaved with a stronghold *shoots straight* with the helper, the person is leveling. Vernon Johnson in his work on alcoholism states:

> To respond openly to being confronted is to *level*. We level when we take the risk of being known by spontaneously reporting our feelings. For example: We level when we let someone know we are hurt—or afraid—or angry.

Using these feelings as an example of leveling is probably useful for two reasons. Anger bottled up, or fear that
is kept hidden seem to lead to more relapses than any
other feelings. Also, anger and fear (along with affection)
are usually the hardest feelings for us to report. . . .

If, instead of leveling, we respond without naming a
feeling, we are hiding.[17]

Intervention

When dependency reaches a point at which people are
hurting themselves and do not know that they need help,
a guided intervention may be necessary. Intervention is
an attempt to change an influencing force that is destroy-
ing a person's well-being.

The principle of intervention is certainly not new since
the Bible records interventions into the destructive
behaviors of many people. Genesis 3 gives an account of
God's first intervention with the first parents of the
human race. After Adam and Eve's act of disobedience
they needed a recovery program, and we have been in
need of recovery since that time. When they hid themselves from God among the trees, he sought a conversation with them asking, "Where are you?" (Gen. 3:9). God
was keenly aware of their fallen condition and obviously
knew their whereabouts but he wanted a response from
them. Through this intervention God helped them see
their condition, held them responsible for their actions,
and provided a way out of their web of deception.

After David took Uriah's wife, Bathsheba, and then had
Uriah murdered in an effort to cover up their sin, the
Lord sent Nathan to intervene in David's destructive
course. Nathan sought a response by telling him about
two men in a certain community: one was rich and the
other was poor (*see* 2 Sam. 12). When a traveler came to
the rich man for a meal, the rich man would not give him
one of his own sheep. Instead, he took the only ewe lamb
that the poor man had, one that had grown up with his
family, and prepared it for the traveler. After hearing the

story David responded with anger toward the rich man, suggesting his death. Nathan then said to David, "You are the man!" (v. 7). Nathan discussed the consequences of David's behavior, and David acknowledged that he had sinned against the Lord. The Lord used Nathan to conduct an intervention on David, helping him see his sinful condition, its long-term consequences, his need for repentance, and how to get back on the track of recovery.

Showing guided level-by-level interventions, Jesus deals with the principle of restoration in Matthew 18:15–17. He begins with an *early intervention* in verse 15. Jesus says: "If your brother sins against you, go and show him his fault, just between the two of you." Early intervention should be done privately, with careful confrontation based on observations (show him his faults), not with judgment and condemnation. This should be done soon after the fault has been observed to prevent delusion. If the brother in the wrong responds favorably, then the issue is over with restoration accomplished.

If the brother does not respond to early intervention, he is probably in a state of delusion. The next step, *intermediate intervention*, is described in verse 16: "'But if he will not listen, take one or two others along, so that every matter may be established by the testimony of two or three witnesses.'" There should be descriptive facts presented based on times, places, people affected, and so forth, as relates specifically to the problem.

The third level of restoration is *crisis intervention*. In verse 17 Jesus says: "If he refuses to listen to them, tell it to the church; and if he refuses to listen even to the church, treat him as you would a pagan or a tax collector." At this level the church should already have a plan in place to assist this person if he is repentant and shows a willingness to receive help. If not, he should be made aware of the church's continued love and compassion for him, but the church members will lovingly detach themselves from him until he shows evidence of wanting to change.

This principle of intervention shows three levels with people being added at each phase. All involved are people who are meaningful in his life. To prevent gossip, it is important to inform only those who need to know. The purpose of intervention is to help people, not tear them down.

How does the local church intervene when a person's addictive behavior reaches a crisis stage? After the individual has been approached with early and intermediate intervention without success, who should be involved in the crisis intervention—the entire church body or just a few meaningful people in the person's life? *A crisis intervention should involve only meaningful people.* Involving the entire local church body would probably include enablers, carnal Christians, and those who do not understand addictive behaviors, which would hamper restoration.

An effective intervention requires much planning since it is a process. Louis B. and Elizabeth Krupnick in their book *From Despair to Decision* present an approach to the process of a guided intervention which I have found to be adaptable to the local church.[18]

First, there must be a time of assessment to gather information about the person, the family, others who care about the individual, and the person who will lead the intervention process. Certain questions should be asked. Do the concerned persons have the emotional stability to be involved in the process and follow-up? Does the information from the concerned persons indicate that the person is dependent and is unable to seek help voluntarily? Is the person who will direct this intervention a caring and compassionate individual? Will the pastor or a member of the pastoral staff be involved to provide spiritual direction? If the interventionist, pastor, and family members decide that a formal crisis intervention may be helpful, then there should be a meeting to help the family understand intervention techniques.

The family members need to understand not only the

dynamics of dependency but also how the entire family will be affected. They should understand codependency (which is discussed later), enabling behaviors, as well as the role defenses and feelings play in the dependent's life. It is important for the family to understand that dependencies will normally get worse before they get better. Since addictive behaviors are progressive, the person is unlikely to get help on his or her own. With life already out of control, the dependent person probably lives in a state of crisis. The family members should understand that a directed intervention is a way for them to begin to take action—at their initiation—with a controlled crisis.

After the family has been educated, an intervention team should be selected. Along with the interventionist, the team can include family members, pastor or member from pastoral staff, employer, social friends, or others who are meaningful in this life. A good-size intervention team is six to eight people. Less than this number may lessen the impact, whereas a larger number of people may lessen the intimacy desired in the meeting.

The intervention should be held at a place where there will be no interruptions. The pastor or counselor's office may be better than the home because there would be fewer distractions. The intervention must be at a time when the dependent person has a sober mind.

One of the most difficult questions may be: How do we get the dependent person to the pastor or counselor's office? I worked with a dependent high school student after he overdosed on drugs over a weekend. In planning for the intervention the parents told the son that they had a meeting planned for him and themselves with me to discuss ways they could help him and the family. The concerned persons should not lie to the individual but insist on attendance at the pastor's or counselor's office and continue until the person responds. After a significant event in life such as an arrest, traffic accident, threatened loss of job, or loss of a friend, the dependent person may be more willing to meet. After all, the person probably knows something is going on because family members have reduced their enabling behaviors.

A preintervention rehearsal with the team will help prepare them for the event. Since participants may experience fear and an uneasiness about the meeting, a rehearsal will help them gain a sense of direction. Each concerned person should be prepared to give written data listing specific dates and events that document the dependent person's powerlessness over an addiction and the concerned person's feelings. The data should not refer to terms such as *dependency, addiction, alcoholic* or *drug addict;* instead, let the facts speak for themselves. (Team members should understand that data documenting child abuse must be reported to proper authorities as required by law.) The rehearsal should close with a summarization and with prayer for God's guidance.

Once the actual intervention begins, the interventionist should explain that all present should hold their questions until each concerned person's data is shared. If the dependent person seeks to sidetrack the data, the interventionist should ask the person to wait until all have shared their concerns. It is important that the data be presented with love and compassion. The information should directly show how the dependent person's behavior affects each of the concerned persons.

After the data is presented, alternatives such as treatment programs or support groups should be presented. It is important that the team has already made arrangements with appropriate alternatives to insure that the dependent person can go for help immediately. The team should be prepared to follow up because the process of recovery has just started.

It should be made clear that if the dependent person leaves the room or refuses to receive help, then family members, pastor, employer, and others who may be on the team will continue to pray for recovery but will no longer offer support until the person chooses to change direction. They are letting the person go, trusting God to get his or her attention.

Relapse

A person who is recovering from a life-controlling problem should always be aware of the possibility of relapse into former ways. The writer of Proverbs says, "As a dog returns to its vomit, so a fool repeats his folly" (26:11). This is particularly true of those who are prone to extreme emotional highs and lows in their walk with God. Some may be overconfident in their recovery process to the point of not guarding against relapse. Crisis situations may trigger a person into relapse. Hidden fear or repressed anger may also lead to relapse.

Goals of Aftercare

Help for a person who is recovering from a life-controlling problem should focus on a vital relationship with God, freedom from the problems that have mastered his/her life, and personal self-esteem. Focusing on a person's relationship with God is a top priority in the individual's recovery.

Sobriety and sober thinking certainly must occur; however, this alone is not enough. Without an ongoing relationship with God a person is likely to switch addictions. For example, Sam has been abstinent from alcohol for six months. However, his introduction to a higher power was void of a personal walk with Christ. Although he was abstaining from alcohol, he switched his dependency to ungodly sexual behaviors. Jesus deals with the principle of an unoccupied spiritual house in Matthew 12:43–45. He says:

> "When an evil spirit comes out of a man, it goes through arid places seeking rest and does not find it. Then it says, 'I will return to the house I left!' When it arrives, it finds the house unoccupied, swept clean and put in order. Then

it goes and takes with it seven other spirits more wicked than itself, and they go in and live there."

In addition to an active relationship with God, there must be continued abstinence or freedom from the life-controlling problem. A person who continues to drink alcohol, use drugs or view R- and X-rated movies (or whatever the dependency is) cannot expect to remain in recovery. Fellowship with God will become strained as delusion once again dominates thinking.

Self-esteem is directly related to the person's relationship with God and personal abstinence or freedom from the problem that has mastered life. Since God is perfect, he is the only one who can communicate personal significance to the person in recovery. Helpers should emphasize the self-worth that comes from being *in Christ* (*see* 1 Cor. 1:30; Eph. 1:3–14; Phil. 1:6; 4:13; Col. 3:3). Paul writes: "In the same way, count yourselves dead to sin but alive to God in Christ Jesus" (Rom. 6:11).

A feeling of being no good or of having no competence can can be a difficult burden for a person struggling on the road to recovery. The helper can encourage the discouraged by helping a person understand that competence comes from a greater power. Paul writes: "Such confidence as this is ours through Christ before God. Not that we are competent in ourselves to claim anything for ourselves, but our competence comes from God" (2 Cor. 3:4, 5).

A person's self-worth will suffer if he or she relapses into a former lifestyle. Since former values will be in conflict with new goals and lifestyle, feelings of failure and difficulty forgiving self will soon surface.

Ways to Attain Goals

An atmosphere of surrender should be encouraged whether it be in a group setting or one-on-one. Individuals who suffer from dependency should be encouraged to live their life one day at a time (*see* Matt. 6:33, 34).

Honesty with themselves, God, and others helps prevent the growth of delusion. They should be encouraged to deal with their feelings and defenses. The helper should encourage persons dealing with relapse to openly communicate with God, asking for his forgiveness. John writes: ". . . But if anyone does sin, we have one who speaks to the Father in our defense—Jesus Christ, the Righteous One"(1 John 2:1). An attitude of humility and responsibility to a local church body that holds the dependent accountable for recovery are essential elements in a recovery program.

Being aware of the various triggering devices that lead to relapse can be helpful to the person in recovery. Paul writes in 2 Corinthians 2:10, 11 "I have forgiven in the sight of Christ for your sake, in order that Satan might not outwit us. For we are not unaware of his schemes." The helper should encourage the person to take a personal inventory of past experiences that enabled the use of a substance or practice to become a mastering behavior. For example some people are tempted to relapse at times of celebration, while others are more likely to fall during times of depression or stress. It is possible that the presence (or absence) of certain people, odors, music, or visual stimulation may contribute to a setback. A person should be aware of these devices and prayerfully take precautions against those things that may trigger a relapse.

Relapse Symptoms

A person who covers up an urge to relapse into a former lifestyle will probably begin to display observable negative behaviors and return to the former state of denial. A first step is to start missing church services or support-group meetings. When I was working in high schools with students who were chemically dependent, there was one sign exhibited by all who relapsed. They would immediately begin to avoid me in the hallways, cafeteria, or at ball games. They would also begin to drop out of their support group.

Socializing with the *former crowd* is another strong sign of relapse. An individual cannot stay straight and continue to *hang out* with former friends who project a negative influence. Being influenced by negative peer pressure will cause a gradual withdrawal from church and support-group friends, although some persons will continue to *talk the talk* but not *walk the walk*.

Ways to Deal with Relapse

It is important to keep communication lines open with those who have relapsed. In an effort to prevent delusion from growing; I would make eye and verbal contact with students who tried to avoid me. Practicing tough love, I would go to their homes when they skipped school and their support group meetings. I would level with them about observable behaviors that concerned me along with supporting data and specific dates.

A person who has relapsed should be encouraged to share feelings about the urge to use a substance or practice a mastering behavior. Encourage the person to continue work on recovery in a local church small group that can offer support and accountability. The helper should set goals of recovery and establish responsibility for meeting them.

Helping individuals who are experiencing hurt behind their Sunday smiles begins with an environment of acceptance and love. Practicing the eight core conditions of helping along with care-fronting sets the tone for an environment of healing and growth. A person is most likely to level in this type of atmosphere. This helps individuals to face the reality of their need for God's help, which is always the first step of recovery from a life-controlling problem or relapse.

3

....

Helping Families
with Dependencies

Immediately after Max concluded his presentation on "Family Dependencies" to a high school faculty, a teacher approached him with tears in her eyes. Margaret, a math teacher, explained that she was a divorcee of three months. Her former husband was controlled by alcohol and compulsive spending. She explained how she was physically and emotionally abused during this ten-year marriage. The couple was in debt to the point of having to declare bankruptcy. Concerned about her children because they were being neglected, she chose a painful divorce to alleviate this family tension.

As the conversation continued, Margaret explained that her father was an alcoholic. As a child she had given much of her time serving as the mom of the family, since most of her mother's efforts and energy were given to her alcoholic husband. Margaret would sometimes help the younger children prepare for school and cook their meals when her mother was not available to care for them.

In this lengthy conversation Margaret finally got to the

point. She said, "Max, you have given a description of my family. With all the pain and suffering I have experienced with my former husband and father I can't believe what I am doing. I have started a relationship with a nice man that accepts me and we are making plans for marriage. Here's the problem! I believe he is also an alcoholic. How could I do this again to my children and myself?"

Whenever a family member has a life-controlling problem, the entire family is affected. These strongholds can be handed down generation to generation if the chain of sin is not broken. Moses writes in Numbers 14:18: "'The LORD is slow to anger, abounding in love and forgiving sin and rebellion. Yet he does not leave the guilty unpunished; he punishes the children for the sin of the fathers to the third and fourth generation.'" "Church and community are concerned with the stability of family life. Family instability contributes inordinately to human suffering 'unto the third and fourth generation.'"[1]

Various theories explain why dependencies run in families. Some experts believe it is hereditary; others contribute it to a person's environment. Frank Minirth, a noted psychiatrist, has said:

> Alcoholism runs in families, but it is not clear whether this pattern relates more to hereditary or environmental influence. If an "addiction-prone" trait is passed genetically, the specific trait has not been identified. . . .
> There is reason to believe that there may be some genetic difference in many but not all alcoholics. But genetics is not the only reason individuals become alcoholics. Nor does every person with this genetic difference become an alcoholic.[2]

Although much attention is given to alcoholism running in families, this is also true of other dependencies. The children of compulsive gamblers learn behaviors that are transferred to the next generation. They have many of the same symptoms that are seen in drug addictions. Child abuse is another problem that runs in families. *"Abusive parents* frequently were themselves abused or neglected in childhood."[3]

Codependency

Mildred walked into her minister's office on Wednesday morning, informing him that she was divorcing her husband, Al. The minister had noticed that she had become indifferent toward the church but he didn't know why. She actually had much to be thankful for because Al received Christ as his Savior thirteen months ago. After experiencing a dramatic conversion, he also had a remarkable recovery from alcoholism.

Prior to Al's conversion, Mildred had regularly asked for prayer for him and often told of her struggles of trying to care for him. She impressed the church with her persistence. Enduring this horrible tragedy of life, she was seen by some as a saint. Brother Hudson had noticed on several occasions in her comments that she seemed to take pride in her suffering.

Mildred took pride in caring for Al's addiction. Her sense of well-being came from being his caretaker. When Al was converted and became sober, her purpose for living seemed to end. His addiction gave her the sense of well-being she needed. Her life was focused on Al versus Christ for her self-esteem. Mildred was codependent.

Shortly after the divorce, Mildred met another alcoholic and later married him. In her quest for self-esteem, she continued the codependent behaviors with her new husband.

Codependency is a popular word used to describe people's behavior when they are addicted to another person. Although this word may be faddish, I do not know of a better term to use. This term surfaced in the late seventies; however the behaviors were in existence long before then. Melody Beattie defines a codependent person as "one who has let another person's behavior affect him or her, and who is obsessed with controlling that person's behavior."[4]

Codependency involves those who take ownership of another person's problem, get a sense of well-being from that person, or allow themselves to be controlled by that person's dependent behaviors. That person's master becomes the friend or relative instead of God. Paul writes in his letter to the Romans: "They exchanged the truth of God for a lie, and worshiped and served created things rather than the Creator" (1:25).

Codependent Relationships

There are certain characteristics that develop in codependent relationships. According to Kathy Capell-Sowder, a person who has a love relationship with an addicted person will demonstrate certain symptoms: increase in tolerance; denial; compromise in value system; major-life areas decline; trapped in the victim's role; plans to escape; addictions develop in other areas.[5]

Increase in tolerance. The excuses from the dependent person are increasingly accepted. The codependent individual experiences an increased loss of control over feelings, mood swings, acceptance of blame, and responses to the addicted person. There is a decline in his or her self-worth along with increased feelings of inadequacy. A wall of defenses designed to help the codependent and other family survive in the relationship to the dependent loved-one is built.

Denial. Feeling the need to protect and cover up for the behaviors of the dependent person, the co-addict joins the loved one in denial. Ignoring the problem and thinking things will get better when they are getting worse contributes to the numbing process of feelings. Codependent individuals deny that their lifestyles are affected by a spouse's stronghold. They may deny their own needs because of their concern for the children. Losing touch with reality, their continued denial results in distorted thinking which leads to a state of delusion.

Compromise in value system. Codependents give much time caring for dependent spouses. Their lack of self-worth may cause problems. They may fall prey to an affair that is totally opposite their values. Their excessive attention given to a spouse may cause the children to be neglected or even abused. Having been raised in church, they may even abandon their commitment to spiritual matters. Betrayal of their value system will increase guilt, causing them to feel unsure about their personal identity.

Major-life areas decline. As the addiction process affects the dependent's emotional, spiritual, and physical well-being, so it is with the codependent. In the co-addicted role a person's emotions are affected by the strain on the marriage. Co-addicted persons begin to doubt themselves and feel the pain over a spouse lost to a life-controlling problem. They may neglect their responsibilities for the children or even abuse them.

Codependents may begin to feel that God does not love them or that they have disappointed God, and there may be feelings of isolation from the Lord. They may experience physical problems including chronic headaches and backaches that are stress related. Employers may notice frequent absences and hospital visits.

Trapped in the victim's role. The impaired thinking of codependents now have them confused without the ability to see their options. They feel trapped because they have lost control of their lives. They don't know how to take options that may be before them because they are in a state of delusion. Co-addictive behaviors have led to an unmanageable life. Feeling trapped, they may sense hopelessness and begin to look for a way to escape from the relationship.

Plans to escape. Codependents may escape by separating or divorcing the spouse. Plans may include having a suitcase packed for departure at all times. They may save money and wait for the children to finish school, then feel free to exit the relationship. Even if they do leave, it may be for only a short period of time, or they may start another relationship with a compulsive person. The co-addictive attachment seems to bring them back to the dysfunctional relationship. They may eventually lose all hope and consider suicide as their way of escape.

Addictions in other areas. Codependents may develop addictions in other areas including gambling, compulsive eating, religion, compulsive spending, or working. Even if codependents exit the relationship with the addicted loved one, they may start another addictive relationship. Codependents become trapped in an addictive system, and it is difficult to break free.

The first step begins with helping codependents break out of their own delusions through awareness. "Overcoming addiction is as much building positive involvements in one's environment as it is withdrawing from addictive attachments."[6] Abstinence or freedom from the life-controlling problem is not enough. A whole new relationship has to be built.

Codependency and Christian Balance

The subject of codependency should be approached with balance. According to Paul, the body of Christ should be interdependent (*see* Rom. 12:7-16; 1 Cor. 12:12-27). Codependency, however, is unhealthy because the person is mastered by a loved one's problem or has become a loved one's master (playing God).

It is possible to live an unbalanced life regarding codependency. On one hand a person may be totally dependent on a friend or loved one for a sense of well-being. On the other hand, an individual may become self-centered in his or her lifestyle without regard for a friend or loved one.

Codependents need to be encouraged to focus on a Christ-centered life versus being addicted to the friend or loved one. The writer of Hebrews says, "let us fix our eyes on Jesus, the author and perfecter of our faith, who for the joy set before him endured the cross, scorning its shame, and sat down at the right hand of the throne of God" (12:2). Codependents should be encouraged to turn their dependency toward God rather than to the dependent friend or loved one.

How to Help a Codependent Person

Helping a codependent move from unhealthy to healthy relationships is a process. Since the codependent is suffering from impaired thinking much like the dependent person, the helper needs to exhibit trustworthiness. Codependents have a low level of trust and need role models who are honest and stable. To be effective the helper needs to display realistic honesty, yet offer hope. Codependents need a helper who mirrors truth, helping them acknowledge obsessive and compulsive behaviors toward the dependent loved one.

The helper should expect codependents to be responsible for their actions. Enabling codependents by mopping up after them or being sympathetic to their self-pity does not help. Codependents need encouragement interacted with accountability. The helper should encourage codependents to be involved in a Christian support group that provides concern, love, and accountability.

Codependents need assistance in understanding the 3 Cs. First, they need to understand that they didn't *cause* their loved one's problem. Many times codependents blame themselves for their loved one's addiction. Feeling they are responsible for the dependent's behavior greatly contributes to codependents' low self-worth. The helper should help codependents understand that their loved one is responsible for the choices that have led to addiction, no matter what the circumstances may be.

Second, codependents need to understand that they cannot *control* their loved one's dependency. It is common for codependents to feel a need to control the loved one's problem by covering up for them or keeping them out of trouble. Trying to control them through manipulation, domination, and guilt only leads to a greater loss of energy. Helpers should assist codependents in understanding that they cannot fix their loved one; instead, they should let go of trying to *play God*. Accepting this fact of powerlessness over the loved one is the first step of recovery for the codependent.

Third, codependents need to understand that they cannot *cure* their loved one. The anger and hurt intensifies as codependents see their inability to cure their loved one through caretaking. Helpers should encourage codependents to cast anxiety on the Lord (*see* 1 Peter 5:7). Codependents need to understand that they are not responsible for their loved one's cure. Since their focus has been clouded by their loved one's behavior, they will probably need assistance in directing their focus toward Christ. Unknowingly their lives have likely become centered around their loved ones to the point of serving them above God. The man of God warned Eli in 1 Samuel 2:29 about this very concern. He said, "Why do you honor your sons more than me?"

Helpers should assist codependents in understanding the importance of focusing on Christ. Their self-identity and freedom comes from being *in Christ*. Codependents need to turn loose their own identity and take on their God-given identity *in Christ*. Jesus says in Matthew 16:24–25: "'If anyone would come after me, he must deny himself and take up his cross and follow me. For whoever wants to save his life will lose it, but whoever loses his life for me will find it.'" Codependents' personal downgrading thoughts of themselves can be transformed into new identity by understanding that their significance comes from being in Christ. Also with this identity freedom and confidence can be gained. Paul writes: "In him and through faith in him we may approach God with freedom and confidence" (Eph. 3:12). As it is with all other human needs, establishing a personal relationship with Jesus Christ is the most effective way in overcoming codependent relationships. Jesus says: "whoever comes to me I will never drive away" (John 6:37).

Children of Dependent Parents

After concluding his sermon on Sunday morning as guest minister, Max was greeted by a young man. With tears flowing down his cheeks, eighteen-year-old Mike presented Max with a tough question. He asked, "What is a normal family?"

He explained to Max that both of his parents were alcoholics. He went on to say that he was converted to Christ one year ago. He had made plans to enter seminary with the assistance of his extended family, his church. Having been raised as a child of dependent parents, Mike had no idea of what a normal family life was like. His church loved him enough to show him God's love, but he still struggled with painful memories.

Forty-year-old Raymond explained to Jim that he had a good marriage. His family was active in church, and he was a successful businessman. He explained that he was thankful for his family because he could not remember ever being a child. His parents sexually abused him and were also alcoholics. Raymond said, "Although I have a good family, I still mourn because I did not have a childhood." Then he asked Jim a difficult question, "How long must I mourn?" Although Jim did not have the answer, he did suggest that Raymond allow God to turn his mourning into compassion for other children of dependent parents.

Various Stages

I have observed that children of dependent parents go through similar stages. Although there has been much written on children of alcoholics—the children of gam-

blers, sexaholics, even workaholics, face similar problems. When a parent is controlled by a life-controlling
problem, there is instability in the home. Gary Collins in
his work on Christian counseling states:

> When parents are not getting along with each other, chil-
> dren feel anxious, guilty and angry. They are anxious
> because the stability of the home is threatened, guilty
> because they are afraid that they may have caused the
> strife, and angry because they often feel left out, forgot-
> ten, and sometimes manipulated into taking sides—which
> they do not want to do. Sometimes there also is a fear of
> being abandoned. Unstable homes, therefore, often (but
> not always) produce unstable children.[7]

Learned behavior. Living with difficult situations, these
children learn to cope with stress. They learn how to protect themselves from possible harm. They learn to not
talk about the problem. The addicted parent is like a big,
white elephant in the living room. Everybody sees him,
but nobody talks about him. Being raised in an unstable
home causes children to lose trust. They learn to suppress their feelings. They become nonfeeling individuals.

Seeking out behavior. During this time of searching, a
caring person may see hints of a problem in these children. They will usually exhibit characteristics of being a
perfect, rebellious, withdrawn, or funny child. In this
stage they may attempt to control their parent's dependency. Delusion sets in and enabling behaviors start in
this stage.

Harmful behavior. The children's compulsiveness will
display forceful defense in this stage. They feel locked in
without strength to make choices. Their behavior becomes a role to deny pain and to cope. They feel responsible for their parent's dependency and blame themselves.
"As we have seen, it is a normal part of the development
process for children to feel that they are the center of the

universe and consequently responsible for the good and the bad things that happen to their friends, siblings and parents."[8] Their painful lifestyle becomes normal.

Escape. Children of dependent parents may act on negative feelings. Escape of the painful lifestyle often results in separation, desertion, or even suicide. As these children approach adulthood they are likely to carry their defensive lifestyle with them to the next relationship. Unhealthy relationships are common among the adult children of dependent parents.

Feelings

Children of dependent parents learn to repress their feelings. To prevent *rocking the boat,* they restrain their emotions. Anger builds as the children move back and forth between a love and hate relationship with their parents. Feeling responsible for their parents, they blame themselves. This self-blame internalizes, bringing on hurt emotions. These children may have low self-worth with shameful feelings.

Their feelings are affected by a life of isolation and loneliness. These children live with the fear of being abandoned by their parents at any moment. They fear the unexpected since their parents' behavior is so unpredictable. For example, the father tells his son he will take him fishing on Saturday. He breaks his promise because he is *hung over* from his alcohol consumption on Friday night. When they receive very little attention, these neglected children experience painful emotions. They feel mixed up, confused, and boxed-in since they are trapped without options that may free them.

Survival Behaviors

Children condition themselves to cover their pain. Concerned about getting their needs met, they may give in to behaviors that betray their values. The oldest child in the family may take on the role of the mother or father in being responsible for the other children. "I've seen five-year-olds running entire families," says Janet Geringer Woititz.[9] These children are known to be loyal to their parents even when loyalty is harmful or undeserved. To protect themselves from physical harm during a parent's drunken condition, some children have been known to sleep with large knives or hammers under their pillows.

Having a need to survive, these children develop certain roles. Usually the *perfect child* takes on the responsibility of the other children. This is often the oldest child. This child is likely to excel in academics, sports, or other school activities and usually becomes a leader in adulthood. Having an unhealthy desire to be perfect, this child needs help in understanding his or her feelings. The *rebellious child* acts out negative feelings and frustrations. In an attempt to get attention, this child will probably resort to antisocial behaviors. The child may turn to drugs as a means of escape. Such a child needs boundaries and should be made responsible for personal actions. It is common for other family members to take out their frustrations on this child.

The *withdrawn child,* usually the middle child, suffers from poor self-esteem. This child is usually a loner with limited self-expectations and has difficulty building friendships. Not knowing where he or she fits in, this child may have difficulty with personal identity. Having difficulty with parental role inconsistency, this child needs help in overcoming fear. Helpers should assist the victim in recognizing personal strengths.

The *clown* is usually the youngest child who has been overprotected by other family members. The child is likely to be immature. Although intelligent, he or she may have difficulty in concentrating. This child needs help in accepting responsibility. Getting caught up in the child's silly behavior is not helpful. Rather, accountability and meaningful self-direction is needed.

Understanding these roles as defense systems is important for the helper. Charles Leerhsen and Tessa Namuth report:

> A high achiever in school, the Hero always does what's right, often discounting himself by putting others first. The Lost Child, meanwhile, is withdrawn, a loner on his way to a jobless adulthood, and thus, in some ways, very different from the Scapegoat, who appears hostile and defiant but inside feels hurt and angry. . . . Last and least—in his own mind—is the Mascot, fragile and immature yet charming: the family clown.[10]

Although much has been written concerning children of alcoholics and the roles they play, these roles also exist in most families. However in dysfunctional systems they are more noticeable since they become coping devices.

Without Help

Without help the children of dependent parents may have a trail of problems. Feeling responsible for everything, they may become workaholics or develop other compulsive behaviors. They are likely to show little zest for life. Having a lack of trust, it is difficult for them to build meaningful relationships. Their potential may never be discovered.

They are likely to marry a dependent person, starting the merry-go-round of problems again. Having no guidelines for parenting, adult children of dependent parents often resort to the ways they were raised. Normal behavior for a functional family is unknown to them. They often make decisions without consideration for the consequences. Judging themselves harshly becomes standard practice.

With Help

With assistance, children of dependent parents can develop functional relationships. Having self-discipline, they can become good leaders, dependable and responsible. They learn to accept responsibility with an understanding of reality. Some of the best role models and creative people are children of dependent parents who have received help. They are normally willing to help others. Although many of the children have lived in horrible conditions, they can learn to let go and have fun.

Ways to Help Family Members

Living in a state of delusion, children of dependent parents have a difficult time seeing reality. Inviting them to share their concerns helps build a trust relationship between the child and the helper. The helper should be a mirror of reality for the victim while modeling honesty. Since the child's needs may have been neglected, the helper should be an active listener. Separating the person from behavior should be practiced by the helper. As with the codependent, the victim should be shown that the child didn't cause the parents' problem, the child can't control it, nor can the child cure it. It is important for the helper to remember that children (and adults) from families with dependencies learn: *don't talk, don't trust, don't feel.*

The church can play a key role in helping families with dependencies. Each family member needs help in developing a healthy relationship. Although a family member may have a dramatic conversion, the addict and the other family members still need support. Having support groups that meet regularly can benefit these people. They can be comforted and learn to comfort others who have similar needs. Paul writes to the church at Corinth: "On him we have set our hope that he will continue to deliver us, as you help us by your prayers" (2 Cor. 1:10, 11).

4

....

A Local Church Model

The Needs and Benefits

The need is alarming. Almost every evening news tele-cast reveals a person whose life has been affected by a life-controlling problem. Family members and friends have been devastated by the behavior. Many people attend church on Sunday morning carrying the baggage of a life-controlling problem. These mastering problems are at epidemic proportions.

Life-controlling problems are like a silent storm with violent destruction. Yes, this storm is in schools, in the workplace, in the home, and it rides on our highways. This silent storm is also in the church family. The results are apparent: fear, hopelessness, and broken family and church relationships.

With this storm comes an opportunity, a tremendous need for the church to get involved. Jeffrey VanVonderen states:

> One-fourth of those surveyed in a 1978 Gallup Poll admitted that alcohol use had negatively affected their

family life. One out of four! At the same time, only 8 percent of all surveyed said they would turn for help to the
church or its trained personnel if they or a family member had a drinking problem.[1]

The local church has more potential to help people
with life-controlling problems than any other agency on
the face of the earth. What other institution, club, self-
help group, or fellowship has the very dwelling place of
the Spirit of God? Paul writes in his letter to the Romans,
"And if the Spirit of him who raised Jesus from the dead
is living in you, he who raised Christ from the dead will
also give life to your mortal bodies through his Spirit,
who lives in you" (8:11).

Leo and Marlene were crushed with pain when their
eighteen-year-old son was arrested for robbery. It was
painful for them because their son had been raised in the
church. He started using drugs at age twelve, but they did
not know where to turn for help. Although they were
faithful members of their church, it seemed to them that
the congregation ostracized them. They felt like people
were avoiding them because of their son's behavior. They
did not have a local church model to assist them in their
sorrow, so they turned to support groups that were not
Christ-centered. They felt even more pain because it
seemed that those outside the church cared more than
the members of their congregation. Actually the congregation cared for them very deeply; they just didn't know
what to say or how to help them.

There are many *walking wounded* Christians that need
the intensive care of a congregation. Having an understanding of the addiction process is important for the
local church. Behind their Sunday smiles, many people
sit in their church pew having already started the addiction process. A local church model that helps people
understand life-controlling problems can intervene in the
early stages of addiction. "It was found that families of
substance abusers . . . *lacked understanding about addic-*

tion and the role it played in the life of the abuser and *tended to react inappropriately to the problem.*"[2]

There are many benefits for the local church that has a model which gives direction in reaching out to people with life-controlling problems. Having such a ministry is expected by the Lord. Isaiah writes: "He has sent me to bind up the brokenhearted, to proclaim freedom for the captives and release from darkness for the prisoners" (61:1). Isaiah further states, "to comfort all who mourn. . . to bestow on them a crown of beauty instead of ashes, the oil of gladness instead of mourning, and a garment of praise instead of a spirit of despair" (vv. 2, 3).

Having a model for the hurting puts the church in touch with America's greatest felt need. Christian love and support can be provided to people who may otherwise look to other sources. Such a model will help the local church fulfill the great commission. Nils C. Friberg in "Health-Giving Church Communities: Biblical Sources and Practical Implications," a paper given at the International Congress on Christian Counseling, states:

> Counseling theory is turning away from sole focus upon individual clients and increasing attention is now being given to human systems and their contribution to either health or pathology. Interrelationship between addictions and family systems, codependency, and the impact of those interrelationships upon children by chemical dependency in parents are now chief foci of human systems studies. These trends make it all the more imperative that we re-examine our theological roots concerning Christian community and its relationship to health on all levels of life.[3]

Discipleship

The conversion experience is only the beginning for the person who has been controlled by a stronghold. My observations show that most people struggle after their conversion. Although there are cases in which some seemingly have no struggles, this appears to be the exception. Victims of life-controlling problems need support in breaking the chains of addiction. They are particularly vulnerable in high-stress situations. Having a crisis situation may cause them to relapse to their former behaviors.

The local church is pleased to see a person controlled by a dependency confess Christ as Savior. With this delight, however, the church should not neglect the family of the new believer. Since the entire family is affected by a family member's addiction, the entire family needs ministry. A whole new relationship should be started. This will require awareness, patience, support, and prayer.

Frank Minirth has noted:

> The *church* ought to be an important resource through which the Christian addict or the addict's family can seek help. These same principles of Alcoholics Anonymous can be used to better advantage when zeroed in on the centrality of Christ. Only within the church or inter-church Christian groups is that likely to happen. Some Christian addicts have been versed enough in their theology to reapply AA's general references to a "higher power" to their previous Christian training and have found their way back to Christ through AA. Other less knowledgeable or less believing Christians have overcome their drinking habits in AA but, in the process, have become doubtful of the importance of Christianity, since it was not what helped them in their hour of need.[4]

Evangelism

Having a local church model that provides principles for reaching out to those who are hurting can be an effective evangelism tool. A congregation that has an air of superiority or makes the addict feel inferior will not be effective. The church that reaches out with acceptance, although with firm love, will stand tall in the community. Their caring will present them with the right to be heard. Paul writes: "If I speak in the tongues of men and of angels, but have not love, I am only a resounding gong or a clanging cymbal" (1 Cor. 13:1).

After the church has established a model for ministering to the hurting, it can consider referrals from court systems, social agencies, places of employment, and school counselors. Ministries can be started on high school and college campuses with the local church model. It is important to understand the position of school officials and board policies. The best approach may be from a serving position versus one's rights to be on campus. A low-key approach with consistency is one way to let our light shine: "let your light shine before men, that they may see your good deeds and praise your Father in heaven" (Matt. 5:16).

Since most prisoners are incarcerated because of a crime committed as a result of an addiction, a felt need can be met in jails and prisons. With each person helped, the door of ministry is opened up to reach entire families. This type of ministry touches American families where they really live. In Matthew's Gospel he writes: "Jesus said, 'It is not the healthy who need a doctor, but the sick'" (Matt. 9:12). Since 15 million Americans are meeting weekly in various kinds of support groups (according to *Newsweek*, February 5, 1990), Christ-centered support groups can be a tremendous tool for evangelism. According to J. David Schmidt (local church consultant) "churches in North America may continue to grow on biological and transfer growth but without a doubt the number-one need of the local church in this country is to discover how to effectively penetrate secular society with the gospel, to provide *doors of entry* into the church for the seeker."

The Value of Small Groups

Small groups are an effective tool that should be used in a local church model for the hurting. Over the past several years I have observed the value of people meeting together to deal with their addictions. J. Keith Miller states:

> The question immediately came up in my mind (and often comes up when people are considering joining such a group): Can people with no theological or psychological training really help each other overcome serious character defects? For years I would have said no. But as I have participated in and watched groups operate over the years I have come to realize that a group of ordinary people trying to surrender their lives to God and discover that their own denial and delusion with rigorous honesty can often give amazingly effective help with real-life difficulties.[5]

Small groups are a way to offer Christian love and support. People are in search of *meaningful relationships.* With Christ as the center of small groups, a therapy can be provided that is not otherwise available. The ultimate therapist is the Holy Spirit.

Loneliness is one of the major problems of our society. Many people are no more than numbers on their jobs. Since a large number of people move from their homes yearly, friendships among neighbors are not likely to be established. With less emphasis on community schools and get-togethers, people feel more isolated. A person may go to church every Sunday without really knowing others that sit in the same pew. That person may be carrying hurts that no one knows about or much less understands.

Small-group ministry can address the problem of loneliness which is even more prevalent among those struggling with life-controlling problems. God deals with man's need for relationships very early in the Bible: "It is not good for the man to be alone" (Gen. 2:18). The Book of Hebrews, which is addressed primarily to Jewish Christians who were tempted to return to Judaism or mix Judaism with the gospel, deals with two important relationships in chapter 10:19–25. In verses 19–23 the author shows the important need for a relationship with God which is provided by the blood of Jesus. In verses 24 and 25 the author discusses the need for a relationship with each other: "And let us consider how we may spur [incite, provoke] one another on toward love and good deeds. Let us not give up meeting together, as some are in the habit of doing, but let us encourage one another. . . ."

Small-group ministry is not a new concept. Jesus' regular meetings with his twelve disciples is a clear example of a small group at work. Not only did the disciples benefit from this experience, but Jesus also received close fellowship with this group. Mark writes in 3:14: "He appointed twelve—designating them apostles—that they might be with him and he might send them out to preach." It is no accident that twelve people or less is suggested for small-group participation.

Christians have met together for almost two thousand years with Christ as the focus and the Bible as the road map. These fellowships have included Bible studies and prayer. Christians have met in homes, churches, and in catacombs. Small groups were active in the New Testament church (*see* Acts 2:41–47). Small groups are not to take the place of corporate worship; their function is to complement the assembly worship. Corporate worship and small groups can provide an environment for spiritual healing and growth. Small groups, where Christ is the focus, are Christian community. When the church is the spiritual hospital, small groups can be the intensive-care unit of the church. Small groups worked together with corporate worship in the New Testament for healthy growth. Luke writes in Acts 2:47: "praising God and enjoying the favor of all the people. And the Lord added to their number daily those who were being saved." Church history records that many of our modern-day denominations originated from small-group ministries.

Small groups can provide a nonthreatening environment for people to receive help in dealing with their life-controlling problems, a place for them to take a look at themselves and focus on practical steps to grow in Christ. Small groups allow a person to be himself or herself, to take off masks, to receive encouragement, to develop accountability to Christ and to one another. According to *Newsweek* (February 5, 1990):

> A 10-year study by researchers at Stanford University showed that terminally ill cancer patients who participated in weekly support-group meetings in addition to receiving treatment lived nearly twice as long as those receiving only medical care.

In small groups, individual prayer and affirmation personalizes ministry. James writes in 5:16: "Therefore confess your sins to each other and pray for each other so that you may be healed. The prayer of a righteous man is powerful and effective." "We need small groups because they help us to become what we are meant to be—those set free by the love of Christ, who seek to share his love with others."[6]

Small groups are one of the most effective ways to deal with delusion. In an atmosphere of surrender to the Lord, the Holy Spirit and Word of God help people see themselves more clearly (*see* Ps. 139:23, 24; Heb. 4:12, 13). God also uses believers to help each other expose delusion through encouragement. The writer of Hebrews writes: "But encourage one another daily, as long as it is called Today, so that none of you may be hardened by sin's deceitfulness" (3:13).

Characteristics of Effective Small Groups

Effective small groups are characterized by Christ's being the *center* of the group. Having a bonding of ideas is good; however, unless Christ is the center, lives will not be transformed. An effective group will be committed to each member and have respect for the claims of Christ.

Commitment to each other means faithfulness in meeting attendance, participation by members, and adherence to confidentiality. In an effective group, each group member will be committed to pray for other group members. Group members take ownership of their feelings without putting others down; they learn to take a look at their own defenses that may be protecting them from the truth.

Effective small groups depend heavily on the group facilitators (leaders). It is suggested that each group have two facilitators. One should take the lead in the meeting and the other should assist in offering input into the group process. The facilitators should work to create an atmosphere for openness and acceptance. Healthy groups develop deep, caring relationships. "One of the basic working assumptions of all group therapies is that human relationships are not only important but also essential for healthy functioning."[7] An effective group experiences learning and growth because Christ, not the group leader or any group member, is the center.

There was a time when aggressive confrontation techniques were used in an attempt to break through a person's delusion. Small groups do not need *four letter words,* shouting or a *tear 'em down* philosophy to be effective. Groups that are effective recognize the value of a Christ-centered environment where there are no put-downs; instead there is respect, nurturing, and careful confrontation.

The Role of Group Facilitators

The role of group facilitators is crucial to the success of groups aimed at helping people with life-controlling problems. The group facilitator and co-facilitator lead the group members, using the appropriate curriculum, through various group dynamics that will change their view of themselves and their world.

There are two things a small-group leader should remember. First, God does not expect the leader to have all the answers or work miracles in the lives of group members. That is God's work. Instead, the leader should simply guide the group toward the healing and solutions which the Holy Spirit provides—God will do the rest. Second, leaders should remember that Christian small groups are quite different from secular ones. Secular groups attempt to bring about *behavior modification* through peer pressure and group dynamics. Although there is a place for positive peer pressure and group dynamics in the Christian small group, there must be a change in the heart. Paul writes: "Godly sorrow brings repentance that leads to salvation and leaves no regret, but worldly sorrow brings death" (2 Cor. 7:10). Behavior modification is only a temporary, superficial solution. God offers deeper, long-lasting change through his body—in this case, the small group. To bring that about the leader must discern the heart of a person's problem and point the sufferer to Christ. In a sense the group leader needs only to *get the ball rolling.*

Healing through the group process will take place naturally. In Matthew's Gospel, he records the words of Jesus, "For where two or three come together in my name, there am I with them" (18:20). Group leaders should be aware of some *dos* and *don'ts* that are important for creating an environment of healing and growth.

Dos. Open each group session with prayer remembering to keep Christ as the *center* throughout the meeting. The main role of the group leader and co-leader is to keep the process going. Although active listening is important, the group leaders should be willing to share their own feelings. This creates warmth and trust which helps group members to feel safe in sharing their feelings.

Care-fronting should always be done with respect and sensitivity. Arrange the chairs so members can easily see each other. Having eye contact will help the interaction. Discussion can be enhanced by open-ended questions. Some examples would be: "Could it be that. . . ." "It sounds like. . . ." "I hear you saying. . . ."

The group leaders should have a sense of humor. It is

easy to get caught up in the seriousness of one another's needs and forget the value of laughter. The author of Proverbs writes: "A cheerful heart is good medicine, but a crushed spirit dries up the bones" (17:22). Humor can enhance the group experience by breaking tension and building trust. Having sensitivity to the timing of humor is important.

Group leaders should have respect for time limitations. The announced time period should be followed. Group members should be respected by the leader starting and concluding the group session on time. Adherence to the agreed time will build respect for the facilitators. It also helps group members to practice discipline as they commit to the time frame of the group.

Group facilitators should always work within their limitations. When the facilitators see an apparent need for professional counseling for a group member, this does not mean that the group leaders have failed nor does it imply that God's power is insufficient. Instead it should be seen as positive because the individual's need has surfaced. In this case the group leaders should ask for pastoral help in determining the most appropriate Christian service available. Each group member's comfort level should always be respected.

Don'ts. Although therapy occurs in Christian small groups led by noncredentialed group facilitators, group therapy, in the professional sense, should not be attempted. Serving as channels of Christ's love to those who are hurting and desire wholeness in Christ is the purpose. Facilitators should not feel it necessary to solve peoples' problems; instead, create an environment in which the Holy Spirit can do his work.

Probing should be avoided since this may open deep emotional wounds with which the facilitators are not prepared to deal. Group members should be encouraged to share their feelings with the understanding that they should not go beyond their *comfort level.* Peter writes:

"Cast all your anxiety on him because he cares for you"
(1 Peter 5:7). Group facilitators should not *interpret* what
group members say, instead, *reflect* what they say.
Counselors who practice group therapy often interpret
what group members say; however, group dynamics is
supportive interaction *between* group members.

Facilitators should not give advice. If the advice given
by the helper does not work, the group member may
hold the person responsible. Advice may hinder the
growth process, since the group members may become
dependent on the group leaders for insight, whereas
active listening assists the individual with a better understanding of self. If a group member seeks advice from a
facilitator, the answer should be general and not violate
biblical principles. Becoming a *caretaker*, accumulating
and owning other people's problems, is not healthy for
the leader or group member. If a group member discloses
information that causes the group leader or members to
feel uncomfortable, it may be appropriate for the facilitator to request a private meeting at a later time.
Facilitators should not feel they must have all the
answers or dominate the group discussion.

Gossip should be discouraged by the group leaders.
Since it is a sin, gossip should not be a part of any group
activity. "In the early church, gossip was condemned and
equated with such sins as slander (2 Cor. 12:20), mali-
ciousness (Rom. 1:29), and idleness (1 Tim. 5:13). It was
assumed that leaders would be free of these characteristics."[8] Gossip will erode the trust level of the group, making it ineffective.

Qualities of Effective Group Facilitators

Having the spirit of a servant is essential for group
leaders. Small groups should not be used as a platform
for building the leader's ego. Leaders must guard against
possessiveness toward group members or manipulation
of those who may be spiritually weak. Christ, not the

group leaders, should remain the focus. A servant's heart can be exhibited by encouraging group members to become all God intended them to be.

Having a good attitude is essential to being an effective group leader. A bad attitude will spread among group members and destroy the purpose of the group. The leader's life should exhibit gentleness, purity, and a loving spirit. Positive attitudes can be as contagious as negative attitudes. Submissiveness to the local church is a quality that is needed for all group leaders. Without submissiveness to each other and Christ, groups will do more harm than good. Paul writes in Ephesians 5:21: "Submit to one another out of reverence for Christ."

Spiritual maturity. Group leaders should have a Bible-based foundation. Paul writes in his second letter to Timothy: "All Scripture is God-breathed and is useful for teaching, rebuking, correcting and training in righteousness" (3:16). Having a good knowledge of the Scripture (*see* 2 Tim. 2:15) along with Bible-based common sense is extremely important. The groups should be led by individuals who are not recent converts (*see* 1 Tim. 3:6). To avoid possible pitfalls, group leaders should be people of proven character. Paul writes: "He must also have a good reputation with outsiders, so that he will not fall into disgrace and into the devil's trap" (v. 7). They should have strong commitment which displays reliability, faithfulness, and follow-through.

Spiritual maturity, gentleness, and humility are a special combination for group leaders. Paul also writes: "Brothers, if someone is caught in a sin, you who are spiritual should restore him gently. But watch yourself, or you also may be tempted" (Gal. 6:1).

Emotional stability. Group leaders should exhibit a balanced lifestyle with confidence, however, not arrogance or overconfidence. Paul says, "For God did not give us the spirit of timidity, but a spirit of power, of love and of self-discipline" (2 Tim. 1:7). Those who cannot discipline their own lives will not be effective in leading others to wholeness in Christ. Leaders should be team players, flexible, and adaptable.

Being responsible people, they should speak and work in reality, never advising group members to stop taking medication or cancel the doctor's care. Small groups are not places to fantasize, exhibit self-punitive characteristics, or heap condemnation on people. S. Bruce Narramore notes:

> A third emotion related to guilt feelings and fears of punishment is what I call constructive sorrow. Paul writes of this in 2 Corinthians 7:9–10, where he reminds the Corinthians there is a difference between worldly sorrow that leads to death and godly sorrow that leads to righteousness. Constructive sorrow is a love-motivated emotion closely related to guilt feelings yet radically different. Whereas psychological guilt is a self-punitive process, constructive sorrow is a love-motivated desire to change that is rooted in concern for others. I believe a confusion of psychological guilt and constructive sorrow has often interfered with the church's efforts at promoting wholeness and health in the body of Christ.[9]

Group leaders who have overcome a life-controlling problem should understand that their purpose is to facilitate learning and growth. They should not put themselves in a position as an expert, based on personal experience. A helper who has been affected by a family member's life-controlling problem should be aware of personal attitudes. Being intolerable to the values and lifestyles of others may prevent group members from receiving the help they need. Stephen P. Apthorp in his clergy handbook on alcohol and substance abuse notes:

> If a recovering alcoholic or recovering drug abuser is selected to be the "spark plug," it must be made clear to him that he is to be a facilitator of people, not a teacher

or an expert witness by virtue of his personal experience. One of the fundamental characteristics of many a recovering person is the need to be in control and the need to control. . . . By the same token, selecting a parent whose child has been impaired by drug abuse may meet the requirements of enlisting a committed person, but in some cases the injury is such that it blocks the person's ability to tolerate others' attitudes, values, or lifestyles.[10]

Communication Skills

Communication skills are extremely important in small-group interaction. "Communication is always occurring in a group for it is impossible for one not to communicate something, either verbally or non-verbally."[11] Effective communications require active listening and having genuine concern for each group member. Since it is easy to develop poor patterns of interacting with people, communication skills require practice.

Open-ended questions help create discussion in the group. These types of questions cause the participants to have a better understanding of themselves. Repeating the content of the group member's message helps individuals know that they are being heard and that you are with them. When confronting is needed, care-fronting skills should always be used.

As mentioned earlier, communications are enhanced by seating arrangements which have people sitting in a circle. Having the need for eye contact, all group participants should be able to see each other. Group members who sit across from each other tend to communicate better than those who sit next to each other. Group facilitators should sit across from each other and acknowledge all contributions to the group process. No one should ever be put down for a comment that is in error.

Group leaders should guard against the temptation to dominate the discussion. It is a common temptation to answer most of the questions, to be the *super* Christian, or to turn the group meeting into a platform for preaching. The leaders should give direction to the group proc-ess by starting the discussion then steer the conversation according to the curriculum being used. It is best to divert conversations on controversial subjects that may cause division among group members. Although the sharing of past experiences can be interesting and in some cases valuable, the focus of the small group should be on the present in the person's life. Since conversation on intel-lectual levels often results in surface discussion, it tends to kill personal sharing. There is a difference between what persons may *think* versus what they *feel*.

Handling excessive talkers in the group. There will be some people who tend to *overtalk* the group or who may wish to show off their knowledge. Some may believe that they have more knowledge than the facilitator (and they may); others may like the attention. There are certain communication skills that can be used to correct this sit-uation. Questions and answers can be directed to indi-viduals by name. Sitting next to the *overtalker* may help since the facilitator receives less eye contact than the other group members. This will cause the person to be away from the focus of attention and be less likely to respond.

The facilitators should analyze themselves to see if they are communicating clearly. If the group leaders are offen-sive, it is possible that the *overtalker* may see the need to take charge. It may be necessary to privately care-front the person. The *overtalker* may have leadership potential but needs to learn to be a better listener.

Handling nonparticipants. Some people are very timid or feel they do not have anything to contribute to the group. There are those who may also have reading diffi-culties. Group participants should be cared for with sen-sitivity (working within their comfort level). There are certain communication skills that can help increase their *comfort level.*

In all group sessions the facilitators should remind participants that no one is expected to disclose if he or she doesn't want to talk. No one is forced to talk—everyone has the freedom to pass. Offering encouragement by gently directing to the shy persons questions that can be answered with ease and comfort will help them become active in the group discussion. These people should receive special attention before and after each group session. Group leaders may need to offer encouragement in private. Every answer they provide should be affirmed.

Phases in Group Life

Understanding the phases in group life is important for group facilitators. "Small groups go through stages as they begin, continue and end their life together. Just as an individual moves through stages in his life from infancy to old age, so groups, too, move through cycles."[12] Although these phases may vary based on the personalities and experiences of the group members, I have observed certain phases that are common with people who are dealing with life-controlling problems.

Trust building. In this initial phase, group participants are building trust in the group and in the leaders. Since group members may not know what to expect, they will be checking the integrity of the group experience. They will have concerns about confidentiality. They will usually discuss surface issues versus their real needs.

During this phase, the group facilitators' task is to develop an atmosphere of acceptance and love. In all go-arounds (a time of sharing for each group member) or exercises, they should first share themselves, which will make group members more comfortable. Group members should be encouraged to share within their own *comfort level.* Participants will need help in seeing each group session as a part of the whole group life. They should be encouraged to be patient in their expectations.

Although the entire group life involves trust building, the first three to four sessions will focus on trust.

Mutuality. In this second phase, emotional involvement deepens among group participants. As bonding among the participants develops, the group begins to take form. Individuals feel more free to express their feelings concerning their personal needs or concerns. Group members begin to share the leadership in the group process.

In this phase, the facilitator's task is to give more attention to the group process. The role begins to change as a leader to that of a facilitator. Being an active listener, the facilitator will need to clarify, reflect, and paraphrase responses from group participants. Since there may be those who may sidetrack the appropriate subject, facilitators will need to tactfully keep the group on the subject.

Affirmation. Group participants will begin to care-front each other with respect and sensitivity in this phase. They will support each other by pointing out the strengths of others and help with one another's struggles. Conflicts that surface should be viewed as a win-win versus win-lose situation, there must be commitment to prayer throughout the group life because unresolved conflict can destroy a group. Group members should understand that commitment to each other means they should disagree agreeably.

Group participants will level within their *comfort zones* which will have significantly increased by this time. Seeing themselves more clearly with the help of others, they will begin to recognize the need to make changes that would please the Lord. Conversation will move from the casual to personal needs. Feeling less threatened, timid members will become more talkative. As the feeling of Christian community intensifies among the group members, participants will begin to value their time together.

Group facilitators need to help the participants focus on the Lord's work in their lives. The writer to the

Hebrews says: "Let us fix our eyes on Jesus, the author and perfecter of our faith" (12:2). With focus on the healing rather than the hurt, facilitators should encourage group members to support each other in love. Those who *overtalk* the group should be tactfully discouraged by the helpers.

Accountability. In this final phase, group members learn to hold each other accountable. Although the group becomes very close, participants begin to develop more individual goals. As spiritual disciplines are developed, identity in Christ arises. They feel better about themselves. New ideas are offered and some individuals may become *preachy.* If the group discontinues its meetings, the members will feel the pain of losing close friends. Termination may cause some to feel abandoned, or they may grieve over the loss of group acceptance and love.

In this phase the facilitators' task is to let go of the need to be the primary help. Participants should be encouraged to be committed to their local church. When the group terminates, leaders should offer encouragement and urge them to remain accountable to others in the body of Christ. "The church is not made of bricks and mortar but of Christians. This fact has a way of being forgotten, and we routinely refer to the buildings where the church meets as 'churches.'"[13] Group facilitators should always encourage group participants to keep Christ as the center of their accountability.

Small Group Format

I suggest that each group session consists of four phases covering a time frame of seventy-five minutes. The four phases are *Introduction, Self-awareness, Spiritual awareness,* and *Spiritual application.* There is a reason for each phase. The facilitators should always plan each session with this format in mind. Quoting Karl Meninger, J. Keith Miller in his work on addiction notes:

The early Christian church cells were comprised of small groups of people who met regularly—often secretly. The order of worship was, first of all, self-disclosure and confession of sin, called exomologesis. This was followed by appropriate announcements of penance, pleas for forgiveness, and plans for making restitution. A final period of friendly fellowship (koinonia) closed the meeting.[14]

Introduction. Begin with prayer. The facilitator may ask one of the group members to lead in prayer. After the prayer, the leader will use a go-around (sharing question) to help get the group at ease and relaxed for ministry. The lead facilitator should respond to the go-around first, followed by the co-facilitator. This causes the group members to feel safer in participating in the exercise. After the facilitators have shared, the group members will share one after another around the circle (go-arounds). Group members should be reminded that they are not expected to share if they wish to pass. The rule is, everyone works within his or her comfort level.

The go-arounds are not for detailed conversation. The facilitator should ask the group to keep comments brief. If a person is obviously in emotional pain during the go-around, the facilitator should interrupt the go-around and have prayer for that individual. After prayer, the go-arounds may resume.

Self-awareness. After the Introduction phase (go-around) is completed, the facilitator will lead the group into the Self-awareness phase. For example, the facilitator may say, "Now it is time for our self-awareness. Tonight we are going to discuss the role of feelings."

Self-awareness is a time to practice James 5:16: "Therefore confess your sins to each other and pray for each other so that you may be healed." It is important to stay on the subject matter. This is a time to focus on needs and healing, not to have a *martyr* or *pity party*.

In the Self-awareness phase the facilitators should ask

the group members to share as they wish, not as in the go-around segment referred to in the Introduction phase. Being at various comfort levels, participants should not feel pressure to self-disclose if they are uncomfortable. As the group continues to meet, members will feel more and more comfortable in being a part of the discussion.

Helpers should always remember, *prayer is in order*. If during this phase a group member is hurting, stop and pray. One of the facilitators may lead in prayer or ask another group member to pray. This says two things to the group. First each member is important. Second the facilitators care about individuals.

Spiritual awareness. After the Self-awareness phase, the facilitator will lead the group into the Bible-study time. For example, the facilitator may say, "Turn in your Bibles to. . . . Our discussion will be on self-control."

Having briefly explained the topic, the facilitator should assign Scriptures to participants who volunteer to read. When each Scripture verse is called for by the facilitator, the group member will read the verse(s). After the verses are read, time should be given to discussion.

Spiritual application. This phase is actually a continuation of spiritual awareness. The facilitator may say, "For our application of the Scripture passage, I would like the group to discuss this question. . . ." The facilitator should ask for volunteers to share reflections on the question. Helpers can assist group members by emphasizing the importance of daily applying biblical principles to their lives.

Small groups, where Christ is the focus, can bring wholeness in Christ to those who are struggling with life-controlling problems. Frank Minirth in a recent work on substance abusers notes:

In our years of pastoral and psychiatric counseling, one of the most effective tools we've found to overcome addictions is believers meeting together, to help each other overcome harmful addictive habits—whether substance abuse, workaholism, TV viewing, eating disorders, or explosive anger. A pastor, therapist, or other trained leader to lead or attend the group is not really necessary.[15]

Although it is true that believers can meet together and help each other overcome life-controlling problems, there should always be an emphasis on spiritual growth. To accomplish spiritual growth it is important for groups to have planned curriculum that focuses on biblical principles. Without goals and facilitators to help implement these goals, the group will probably lack direction and may even develop a sickness mentality ("I am sick and will always be sick").

Help for an individual with a life-controlling problem begins with truthful thinking (thinking that yields to biblical principles). Paul writes in Romans 12:2: "Do not conform any longer to the pattern of this world, but be transformed by the renewing of your mind. . . ." As persons begin to change behavior, in obedience to God's Word, they will begin to experience right feelings. Although the development of a better understanding of one's self (self-awareness) is important, growth in Christ (spiritual awareness and application) should always remain the primary focus.

First John 3:18–20 provides the principle of facts, faith, and feelings which helps us understand this process. First, the person should understand the *facts*. John writes (v. 18): "let us not love with words or tongue but with actions and in truth." Are our love and actions based on truth—on God's Word which is true (*see* Ps. 119:160)? Jesus Christ is actual, factual, and truth (*see* Acts 1:3).

Second, a person's *faith* should be placed on the facts of God's Word. John writes: "we set our hearts at rest in his presence whenever our hearts condemn us. For God is greater than our hearts, and he knows everything" (1

John 3:19, 20). Faith is accompanied by action (*see* James 2:17). To walk in faith a person sets thoughts and feelings at rest in God's Word. Third, a person's *feelings* will conform to the truth of God's Word. John writes: ". . . if our hearts do not condemn us, we have confidence before God" (1 John 3:21).

It is important to rest in God's promises when thoughts and feelings of condemnation come. (If an individual is not walking in truth he or she should immediately get things worked out between himself or herself and God and get on with recovery.) *Feelings* are not the foundation of the Christian walk. Even after walking with the Lord for a long period of time, feelings may bring condemnation at which time a person will need to apply faith to the facts, then rest in God's presence. John writes: "But if we walk in the light, as he is in the light, we have fellowship with one another, and the blood of Jesus, his Son purifies us from all sin" (1 John 1:7).

Organizational Mechanics

Having a local church model for people with life-controlling problems requires organization. To effectively use laypeople in ministry to those that are hurting, the church should provide a system and methodology that helps activate skills and concern. Along with the interpersonal skills and a model, helpers will need various tools, including training and curriculum, to assist them in activating the helping relationship.

Aspects of the Model

For the model to be effective the pastor must offer his full support. The pastor (or pastoral staff) should endorse it in public, show up at early meetings, and offer encouragement to the effort and vision. Although the pastor may not be involved in the ministry activities, the model must stay under his *spiritual covering*. The minister oversees, a coordinator leads, and the Core Team manages.

At full maturity the core group oversees the model which has six components. [*Note:* This ministry model is presented in Turning Point Seminars. Curriculum for Insight Group, Concerned Persons Group, and other related material is available to churches after attendance at a seminar. For information please write: Dr. Jimmy R. Lee, P.O. Box 8936, Chattanooga, TN 37411.]

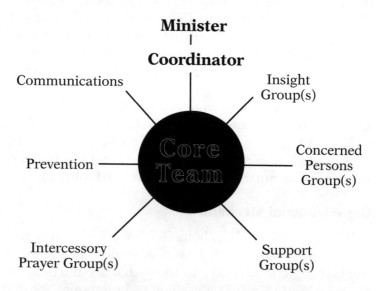

Figure 1: Local Church Model

The Core Team. This is a group of laypeople in the local church who are trained to work with youth, adults and families within the church and community. The laypeople are trained to work as a team to develop small groups which address individuals with life-controlling problems and people who are concerned about their family members or friends. As a team the laypeople coordinate the program as a ministry to the local church body and to those in the community. The Core Team works cooperatively with the minister of the local church they serve.

Each member of the Core Team should have a responsibility. The Core Team coordinator schedules the core group meetings and is the contact person for the minister. The coordinator serves as the representative of the Core Team. Stephen P. Apthorp in his clergy handbook on alcohol and substance abuse notes:

> Since we do not want to be responsible for the process itself, the extent of our involvement at this level is to select a "spark plug," a self-motivated starter, who will assemble this company. The success of an effective chemical-health program depends on who we ask to be that "spark plug." The person or persons will be, in effect, the lay equivalent of the minister. . . . What is vital is that this person be a facilitator of learning and growth more than an imparter of information."[16]

Some team members will serve as they are needed as leaders of small groups. Those who assist with communications will help present the goals of ministry to the church and community. Members who serve in the prevention component provide program and materials for Sunday school classes, youth groups, parents, and community.

Why is a Core Team needed? Because teamwork is important. Without the team approach, helpers are likely to become overburdened which can lead to burnout. It is impractical to think the ministerial staff alone can deal with the hurts and staggering needs that most congregations face. In truth this work should be the responsibility of the entire local body of Christ. Churches in New Testament days were built on the assumption that believers would minister to each other. We can learn from this example and become people helpers. The Core Team should be respected by the congregation, trustworthy, and committed to Christ. They should be good role models, enthusiastic, positive, compassionate, and persistent.

Following the example of Christ's earthly ministry, there should be a team approach to ministry. In Mark

3:14 we read: "He appointed twelve—designating them apostles—that they might be with him and he might send them out to preach."

There is strength in numbers. A team of people dividing the responsibilities of helping hurting people can help more efficiently than one person who is trying to do everything. Helping people with life-controlling problems is a big job—too big for one person.

The team approach to ministry benefits not only those who are being helped, but also benefits those who are doing the helping. Persons serving Christ on a Core Team will experience the joy of helping others, and will also experience the encouragement and support of fellow team members. What a comfort to know that others are there to help with tough problems, to encourage them to be faithful to their calling, and to pray for them specifically.

To meet the varied and specific responsibilities of the Core Team, look for persons with these characteristics:

The Core Team Coordinator must be an organizer and delegator. This person loves to organize people and projects and is probably a list maker. A delegator knows when to ask for help and who to ask.

The Prevention Coordinator must be an idea person and a resource person. This person is full of suggestions for everything from family Christmas gifts to raising funds for the homeless. A resource person loves the library and takes joy in matching a person with a helpful book.

The Intercessory Prayer Coordinator must be a faithful prayer warrior. This person doesn't just talk about prayer, but prays daily because he or she believes prayer makes a difference.

The Communications Coordinator must be a good communicator. This is someone who doesn't mind standing in front of others and giving a short, motivating announcement.

Insight Group, Concerned Persons, and Support Group Facilitators must have these characteristics: a vibrant spiritual life, servant heart, positive attitude, consistent track record, listening ear.

The Core Team should meet at least once every two weeks. Having an agenda carefully prepared by the coordinator helps to keep the meetings on target. The agenda should include a word of encouragement and a passage of Scripture. Other items should include a progress report from each small group, discussion about new groups, and a report from those responsible for prevention. The meeting is a time to pray for specific needs and give support to each other. Needing teamwork and support, the Core Team should plan fun activities together. Ten to fifteen Core Team members is sufficient; however, a very large church may need thirty to forty helpers.

Insight Group. This small group is for those who need help to stay free from life-controlling problems. Primary candidates for this group are people who have made a commitment to Jesus Christ but need support in staying free from a life-controlling problem. Those who want help but have not committed themselves to Christ may also be placed in the group. The love and acceptance of the group may help point them to Christ as Savior.

The Insight Group should meet for seventy-five minutes one time per week. The group is designed for nine sessions, but may go longer if necessary. At the conclusion of the course each group member should be encouraged to continue in a *Concerned Person's Group* or an ongoing *Support Group* (*see* Appendix 1).

The Insight Group facilitators should follow the small-group format discussed earlier (pp. 112-13) to deliver the curriculum content (*see* Appendix 2 for outline of Insight Group). The curriculum should be designed to help the participants (through self-awareness) take a look at their delusions. The self-awareness phase should include discussions of trust, feelings, defenses, the stages of addiction, and the symptoms of life-controlling problems. In the later stages of the group life, participants should be given the opportunity to evaluate each other's progress and struggles. The aim of the evaluations should be encouragement.

The spiritual awareness and application phases should center on biblical passages along with practical application. Peter mentions eight objectives in his second letter that have practical usage for the Insight Group. Peter writes: "For this very reason, make every effort to add to your faith goodness; and to goodness, knowledge; and to knowledge, self-control; and to self-control, perseverance; and to perseverance, godliness; and to godliness, brotherly kindness; and to brotherly kindness, love" (2 Peter 1:5, 7). In the first session, the facilitator should lay the groundwork for this passage. Starting with session 2, each of the eight objectives should be discussed one by one over a period of eight weeks or more. It is important to stress to the participants that if the eight objectives are progressively developed, they will render each person useful and fruitful in serving Christ.

During the first session (orientation), goals and ground rules for the group should be discussed. Emphasis should be placed on confidentiality and commitment to the group meetings. Each participant should be asked to commit to abstinence from nonprescribed drugs and alcohol. If a participant continues to use such substances during the group life, he or she is not likely to receive help because of delusion. If genuine efforts are made to abstain without success, treatment may be needed for addiction. If participants cannot deal with behavioral addictions, they may need the care of a professional Christian counselor.

Care for people with life-controlling problems should address the whole person. Paul helps us understand the uniqueness of the whole person in 1 Thessalonians 5:23: "May God himself, the God of peace, sanctify you through and through. May your whole spirit, soul, and body be kept blameless at the coming of our Lord Jesus Christ."

A person's body is weakened by life-controlling problems. The soul, which involves the mind, emotions, and will, loses touch with reality. As the mind and emotions become callous and deluded, the spirit has difficulty relating with God. Although the soul and the spirit are thought of as being together (and there are many Scriptures to support this), each has distinct aspects that helps us understand the inner being. Regarding these aspects, the writer of Hebrews states (in 4:12), "For the word of God is living and active . . . it penetrates even to dividing soul and spirit."

Humans make contact with the physical world through the body. This body, which houses the soul and spirit, is described as a human tent (*see* 2 Cor. 5:1; 2 Peter 1:13, 14). Causing much pain and suffering, life-controlling problems can be devastating to the human body. It comes as no surprise that the so-called sexual freedom (sex outside the boundaries of marriage, homosexuality, incest) is responsible for many sexually transmitted diseases that plague our society. With many life-controlling problems in the church at Corinth, Paul writes in 1 Corinthians 6:19–20: "Do you not know that your body is a temple of the Holy Spirit, who is in you, whom you have received from God? You are not your own; you were bought at a price. Therefore honor God with your body."

The soul (or self) consists of the mind, emotions, and will. Everything a person knows is stored in the mind (intellect). Perhaps the greatest struggles with a dependency is in the mind (deluded thinking). A person's emotions become entrapped, causing behavior or feelings that bring enslavement. The person may lose the power to make choices or decisions. Paul says in 2 Corinthians 10:4, 5: "The weapons we fight with are not the weapons of the world. On the contrary, they have divine power to demolish strongholds. We demolish arguments [imaginations] and every pretension that sets itself up against the knowledge of God, and we take captive every thought to make it obedient to Christ." Paul also discusses the importance of having a renewed mind (*see* Rom. 12:2; Eph. 4:24; Col. 3:10).

We make contact with God through the spirit (*see* John 4:23; Rom. 8:16). God warned Adam in the Garden of Eden that he would die if he ate from the forbidden fruit. When he ate of the tree, he died immediately spiritually (*see* Gen. 3) and later died physically (*see* Gen. 5:5). We are spiritually dead (separated) without Christ; however, when we receive Christ as Savior, we are granted a new birth (*see* John 3). After the new birth we are encouraged to "grow in the grace and knowledge of our Lord and Savior Jesus Christ." (2 Peter 3:18).

Since we have the potential of being in contact with the spiritual world, we can be influenced by forces that are not in agreement with Christ as the Son of God. The term *spirituality* is commonly used in circles unrelated to biblical truths especially in the addiction field, where there is an influx of New Age thinking. John warns in 1 John 4:1: "Dear friends, do not believe every spirit, but test the spirits to see whether they are from God, because many false prophets have gone out into the world."

God brings about change in us from the inside out. Our spirit must come in contact with God through Christ before there can be lasting change and fulfillment. Jesus says: "For from within, out of men's hearts, come evil thoughts, sexual immorality, theft, murder, adultery, greed, malice, deceit, lewdness, envy, slander, arrogance and folly. All these evils come from inside and make a man unclean" (Mark 7:21-23).

The Insight Group is the place for participants to take a close look at their life through self-awareness. Self-awareness is not enough; they need spiritual awareness which helps in their relationship with God. A balanced approach is important for these people because God uses helpers to break the chains of life-controlling problems and deluded thinking. Frank Minirth notes:

God has given us the power of choice to live our lives to his glory or to ourselves and our own degradation. Choosing to live to his glory also means choosing to keep ourselves healthy in the physical, mental/emotional, and spiritual areas—body, soul, and spirit—of our lives. . . .

Body—knowing and taking care of our bodies, which are houses and temples for soul and spirit—ours and God's.

Soul—gaining insight into ourselves and growing in that insight.

Spirit—knowing the Lord and growing in him.[17]

Concerned Persons Group. This small group primarily is for those who want to help someone close to them who is enslaved by a stronghold. This group is also for people who are suffering the consequences of a loved one's life-controlling problem. Quite often these participants are struggling with very sensitive and emotional issues. These people need compassion and comfort. Paul writes: "Praise be to the God and Father of our Lord Jesus Christ, the Father of compassion and the God of all comfort, who comforts us in all our troubles, so that we can comfort those in any trouble with the comfort we ourselves have received from God" (2 Cor. 1:3, 4)

The purpose of this group, then, is to encourage and strengthen each group member in God's love. Group facilitators should exhibit love, honesty, and respect without being judgmental. I suggest that all Concerned Persons Group members complete the Insight Group as a prerequisite to this group. Attendance in an Insight Group prior to the Concerned Persons Group helps to prepare the participants for this group. Even though they may want to learn how to help as a concerned person, participation in an Insight Group helps them begin the process by looking at themselves first. This group should meet once each week for seventy-five minutes over a period of nine weeks.

Group facilitators should follow the small group for-

mat (*see* pages 112-13) in applying the curriculum content. The self-awareness should include discussions on
hope, codependency, enabling behaviors, family emotional stages, care-fronting and the role of feelings and
defenses. Knowing the various needs for support, facilitators should offer comfort to each group member along
with encouragement to grow in Christ (*see* Appendix 3).

In the spiritual awareness and application phases
emphasis should be placed on biblical principles that
apply to the needs of concerned persons. They usually
feel burdened down with the loved one's problem. Some
will be addicted to a relationship with a friend or loved
one. The facilitators should use biblical principles that
deal with codependency, powerlessness, hope, self-worth,
and enabling behaviors. Having stuffed their feelings,
participants need assistance in getting in touch with their
emotions and support for self-esteem. Focus should be
centered on the members receiving their self-esteem
through Christ. Paul in his letter to the churches at
Galatia writes: "I have been crucified with Christ and I no
longer live, but Christ lives in me" (Gal. 2:20). Paul also
discusses the importance of being in Christ in his letter to
the church in Ephesus. He writes: "In him we have
redemption through his blood, the forgiveness of sins, in
accordance with the riches of God's grace" (Eph. 1:7).

New members should not be added to the Insight or
Concerned Persons Group after the second meeting.
When the group is interrupted with new members, the
progress of the group is slowed, and the new member
may not feel a part of the group.

To handle the continuing influx of new members,
Insight and Concerned Persons groups should be started
at staggered times. For example, one Insight Group and
Concerned Persons Group could start today. The next
group would begin in three or four weeks. People wanting to join a group between start-up times can be
assigned to a Support Group (topical study) until the
next group starts.

Support Group. The Support Group is for participants who desire continued help, having already been through the Insight Group and Concerned Persons Group. "Most small groups last for about two years if they decide to continue after the initial eight to ten weeks."[18] With the experience of having been through the Insight and Concerned Persons groups, participants will understand the self-awareness and spiritual awareness phases. Facilitators may select the appropriate curriculum for the Support Group. Choices may include a Christ-centered twelve-step program, Sunday school curriculum, or a specialized study for the spiritual awareness.

Intercessory Prayer Group. This group meets weekly to pray specifically for the minister, congregation, and those involved in the helping ministry. Helping people with life-controlling problems is a spiritual warfare. Paul writes in Ephesians 6:12: "For our struggle is not against flesh and blood, but against the rulers, against the authorities, against the powers of this dark world and against the spiritual forces of evil in the heavenly realms." Charles Stanley in his work on prayer states:

> It is time we quit struggling against flesh and blood and deal with the real enemy. We have only one weapon. It is not preaching, teaching, singing, or organizing; it is the Word of God brought against Satan's lies through prayer. Our prayers build the Kingdom of God and destroy the Kingdom of Satan.[19]

Prevention. Those Core Team members involved in prevention serve as a resource for the various ministries of the church. Their primary focus is to provide healthy alternatives based on biblical principles of living for youth and adults. For example programs can be presented on how to *say no* to substances and behaviors that may enslave a person. Paul writes in Titus 2:11, 12: "For the grace of God that brings salvation has appeared to all men. It teaches us to say 'No' to ungodliness and worldly passions, and to live self-controlled, upright and godly lives in this present age." The primary institution to deal with the prevention of drugs, AIDS, abortions, and premarital sex is the family and the local church, not the schools.

Communications. The Core Team members involved in communications present the goals of the helping ministry to the church and the community. They inform the congregation when and where small groups will meet. They also assist group members in signing up for the appropriate group. Announcements on a church bulletin board and in church newsletters can be effective in getting the *word out*. Television and radio advertisements are useful in getting the ministry known among the community. Visits to social agencies, school counselors, and judges can result in referrals to the local church helping ministry. Printed materials that describe the ministry should be given to interested agencies. Announcements and advertising helps to inform people; however, the personal invitation remains the best form of communication.

The Legal Aspects

With the heightened litigation mood of America, churches should take certain precautions in their ministry to people with life-controlling problems. Helpers should focus on spiritual versus psychological care. From a clearly written statement, participants should know what they can expect in small-group activities. The statement should explain that the approach is primarily spiritual and biblical rather than simply psychological or physiological. Here is an example:

> *Please understand that this ministry is not a substitute for medical or psychological care. We never advise anyone to stop taking medication or cancel the doctor's care.*
> *We give our time, compassion, and love solely as caring people who want to be channels of Christ's love to those*

who are hurting and desire wholeness in Christ. As non-credentialed persons, we promise no professional psychological expertise.

Although it may not be intentional, group facilitators should never deceive participants with misleading claims. These claims may be concerning a leader or the group's ability to solve a participant's problem. The focus should always remain on Christ and biblical principles. Misleading claims can be avoided by following a set curriculum for each session. Having two facilitators reduces the possibility of one leader becoming the *spiritual* or *psychological guru.*

Confidentiality should be explained during the orientation session of the group life. "Confidentiality refers to the act of protecting from disclosure that which one has been told under the assumption that it will not be revealed without permission."[20] During the discussion regarding confidentiality, the facilitators should discuss the ground rules of confidentiality. Confidentiality will be broken if people are a danger to themselves or to others (for example, the revealing of suicidal tendencies or the reporting of child abuse). Second, the pastor has privilege to the confidentiality of the group. Being the spiritual leader of the congregation he should have privilege to this information if he so desires or the facilitators deem it helpful.

Group leaders should beware of their limitations. Some participants may need the care of professional Christian counselors. There are certain elements that facilitators can use as indicators. If a person has a long history of firmly rooted problems or if a person shows signs of repressed memories, he or she may need professional care. Those who have strong tendencies toward self-punishment and condemnation can be difficult to work with. Some may not have clearly defined problems or they may be tormented with deep depression. A person in the group who is struggling with an addiction and

shows no signs of abstinence (even temporary abstinence) may need the care of a treatment program. Group
facilitators should, in consultation with their minister,
offer various referral options from which participants
may choose. "The pastoral or lay counselor should con-
sistently and readily seek advice regarding any phase of
the counseling process."[21]

Evaluating Professional Counseling: Christian or Secular

When a person needs to receive professional counseling or enrollment in a support group should the options
include secular help or only those who counsel from a
biblical perspective? To answer this question we first
need to take a quick look at the trends in our society over
the past twenty years.

During the last two decades American values have
eroded because our nation has chosen to move away from
its Judeo-Christian roots. Prayer is no longer permitted in
public schools, nativity scenes have been removed from
public property, and there has been increased defiance
toward the Bible. New Age thinking has increased, pro-
moting a philosophy that directly opposes Jesus' statement that he is "the way and the truth and the life. No
one comes to the Father except through me" (John 14:6).
This statement is regarded as being narrow-minded, may
be okay for those who choose it but not the truth for
everyone.

Although the twelve-step program of Alcoholics
Anonymous finds its origin in biblical principles, caution
must be taken because New Age thinking has moved into
many twelve-step programs. Spirituality is discussed in
nebulous, nonspecific terms. For a person who is not
familiar with Christianity, a personal interpretation of a
higher power may be Buddha, Mohammed, a lover, or
nature. The Bible teaches there is only one way to God
and the route is through his son, Jesus. All other roads to

God will end in emptiness and death. John records the words of Jesus in John 10:1: "the man who does not enter the sheep pen by the gate, but climbs in by some other way, is a thief and a robber." Jesus describes the thief in verse 10 as one who comes "to steal and kill and destroy." Dr. Gary W. Sweeten has developed a Christ-centered twelve-step program called "The Twelve Steps to Wholeness" (see Appendix 4) which places Christ in his rightful position as Savior and healer.

Several questions need to be addressed in choosing a counselor. Does the counselor believe that man is born a sinner or does the counselor hold that man comes into this world good? David declares in Psalm 51:5: "Surely I was sinful at birth, sinful from the time my mother conceived me." Does the counselor exhibit an understanding of the sinful nature? Does the counselor believe that through Christ the counselee can be freed from the dominion of sin? Paul writes in Romans 6:14: "For sin shall not be your master, because you are not under law, but under grace." Has he received Christ as his personal Savior (see Rom. 10:9, 10)?

How does the counselor regard the work of the Holy Spirit in counseling? Is the Holy Spirit identified as teacher and guide (see John 14:26; 16:13)? Is the Bible viewed as the final authority in counseling techniques and practice? Paul writes in 2 Timothy 3:16: "All Scripture is God-breathed and is useful for teaching, rebuking, correcting and training in righteousness."

Finding the appropriate counselor may be difficult. However, the helper should be a person who uses the Scripture as the "truth test" because all truth comes from God. Any teaching or practice that is in conflict with the Bible is in error. Paul warns: "See to it that no one takes you captive through hollow and deceptive philosophy, which depends on human tradition and the basic principles of this world rather than on Christ" (Col. 2:8).

The first test for seeking out a counselor or support

group should be the "truth test." Helpers should be Christian in testimony (John 3:3) and practice (Col. 2:6, 7), not only in name. A good question to ask a counselor or group leader is the question Jesus asked the Pharisees in Matthew 22:42: "What do you think about the Christ? Whose son is he?" The answer to this question will help the counselee determine the helper's point of reference.

If competent Christian counseling (not every claim that comes under the name of Christianity is competent or is Christ-like in practice) is not available, where does one go for help? If people choose to go to a secular counselor they should also remain accountable to the pastor, a member of the pastoral staff, or a layperson to insure that they are not being led astray by secular philosophy. Spiritual direction should come from the local church that is Christ-centered in doctrine and practice.

Getting Started

I suggest that the minister select a coordinator and Core Team to start a ministry for the hurting. Almost every church has a group interested in this type of ministry. The group should receive specific training. After the training, the Core Team should participate in an Insight Group together before the members actually start the functions of the team. Attending the Insight Group is important for three reasons: 1. Helpers should be aware of their own spiritual and emotional needs. 2. Attending the Insight Group sends an important message to the congregation: *This ministry is for everyone*. 3. Helpers receive on-the-job training.

An effective ministry that will help people at all phases of life-controlling problems should be focused toward the mainstream of the congregation. I have observed that in the typical evangelical congregation, 20 percent of the people do most of the work and are usually committed regardless of circumstances. Another 20 percent struggle with immense problems that affect their relationship with God and their commitment to the local church body. The remaining 60 percent are the mainstream, some are being affected by life-controlling problems. However, they do not see them as problems. Others may be concerned about a life-controlling problem but they deny its existence to others.

The deniers in the mainstream segment of the church are more likely to get involved since they are not labeled as being addicted, dependent, or sick. The 20 percent who do most of the work will likely be involved if the ministry is promoted as discipleship, and many of the 20 percent who are struggling will also participate because their problems are already at a mastering phase.

To prevent labeling, the Insight Group, which is the entry group for all participants in the small-group process, deals with addiction in generic terms. No specific addiction is highlighted because the dynamics of most dependencies are the same regardless of the type (drugs, alcohol, sex, gambling, eating disorders, and so forth). This helps the church develop a more acceptable and sensitive environment for those who may not want to be identified as having a problem—even though they may. This approach helps to avoid the stigma of the ministry being only for "sick" people since it targets everyone in the church.

Using this approach should assist the local church body to deal with traditional church attitudes that create resistance toward helping the hurting. Certain myths contribute to resistance. One of the greatest myths concerns the term *life-controlling problem*. To some people, this description conjures up extreme images: an alcoholic passed out on the floor after a drinking binge; a heroin junkie scrambling for another fix; a nymphomanic hopping from bed to bed. To some people life-controlling problem is just another name for addiction.

These people may not recognize the fact that life-controlling problems include such general life areas as unhealthy relationships and perfectionism. They may not understand how the family is affected by a family member's life-controlling problem. Many difficulties that surface in the local church may find their root in a life-controlling problem. To view this ministry model as a program for addicts is to lose sight of the wide-reaching scope of the ministry and potential ministry participants.

After participants have completed the Insight Group they then should participate in a Concerned Person's Group. Since most people have a concern about a friend or loved one's problem or are affected by the consequences of a significant other's behavior, the Concerned Person's Group will provide a greater awareness and support for them. After completing the Concerned Person's Group they may need continued participation in an ongoing support group that addresses a specific need. For example, see Appendix 5 "Small Group Flow Chart."

To keep the momentum going in your church, this model is designed to be—and works much more effectively as—a *process,* not a disjointed erratic series of small-group studies. (Thanks to J. David Schmidt for assistance on how to keep the momentum going in the local church.) Three elements are necessary for implementing a "process" mind-set in the ministry: *a master plan, continuous new leadership training, and communication.*

Before a ministry can have a "process" mind-set, it must have a complete, prayerful assessment of *where it wants to go.* A master plan is needed. The plan must be in tune with the specifics of the ministry. Factors such as the number of ministry participants, the number of available leaders, and calendar schedule must be considered.

The plan should be comprehensive and detailed. In drawing it up, ministry leaders should consider every question that might be asked about the ministry:

"What if a leader is unable to be at a meeting?"
"How and when will we train new leaders?"

"How will we promote the ministry?"
"What options will group members have when they
complete a small group study?"

Not only should the plan be comprehensive and
detailed, it should also be flexible. It is impossible to fore-
see everything that might occur within the ministry. And
just because something is planned, it doesn't mean it will
occur. And just because something is planned, it doesn't
mean it will occur as expected. Provisions and alternatives should be built into the plan to account for the natural processes of turnover and attrition. By the same
token, flexibility in the plan will allow ministry leaders to
take advantage of opportunities that arise.

One of the obvious by-products of a "process" mentality is ministry growth. And as more and more people join
the ministry, the need for leaders increases. Therefore a
process mentality is impossible without continuous, new
leadership training. Leaders of the ministry should
always be on the lookout for potential leaders. Every
ministry participant should be assumed to be a potential
leader until proven otherwise. Once a viable leadership
candidate is identified, that person should be encouraged
and trained.

If this model of ministry is to be viewed as a "process,"
it must be communicated as such. Not only must the
master plan be created, it must also be *communicated* to
the congregation. People interested in the ministry must
recognize from the beginning that it is not a one-time
occurrence. Promotion can also be used to relate information to those interested in becoming leaders. A steady
flow of such information is bound to yield dividends.

A master plan, continuous new leadership training,
and communication—when used effectively together—
they can transform a disjointed, stop-and-start ministry
into a *process*.

Initial Promotion

The best way to promote this type of ministry in your church initially is simply word of mouth. The Core Team Coordinator and the pastor should contact people they think would be interested in being a part of the Core Team. A pulpit announcement may be appropriate.

Once the Core Team is established and ready to launch Insight Groups, your promotional needs will change. Although word of mouth will continue to be your best advertisement, here are suggestions on how to promote the ministry model throughout your congregation:

An announcement from the pulpit:

Did you know that for every twelve people in a church pew, at least three suffer under the weight of a life-controlling problem? life-controlling problems include: eating disorders, unhealthy relationships, perfectionism, addictions to various substances and behaviors, and so forth. A life-controlling problem is anything that masters our life. Paul writes in 1 Corinthians 6:12:"I will not be mastered by anything." We recognize that everyone has the potential of having a life-controlling problem. Paul also states: "I am not ashamed of the gospel, because it is the power of God for the salvation of everyone who believes" (Rom. 1:16).

We are in the process of launching a ministry to help those struggling with such problems. This ministry [your ministry name], relates the power of Scripture to where people are and gives them practical handles for release from their problems. If the church is a hospital, think of [your ministry name] as the intensive-care unit.

Notice the insert in your bulletin. This ministry is not just for those struggling with a life-controlling problem themselves, but for anyone wanting more insight into life-controlling problems—how they can be prevented, and how the truths of Scripture relate.

Join us [date, time, and location] for a brief meeting that will answer all your questions about this ministry.

Commitment Encouraged

Since there can be various obstacles, there must be a high level of commitment from the Core Team. Some people may resist the ministry because of personal biases. The comments may range from "ain't it a shame nothing can be done" to "only professionals can do this kind of ministry." To be successful the ministry will need the same priority given to other important ministries of the church.

Persistence Required

It may take some time to start a helping ministry for people with life-controlling problems. Since some people in the congregation may view the ministry as another fad, persistence will help build credibility. Some people will take the "wait and see" approach. They may need support, but it may take time to gain their confidence so they will seek out support. The ministry must be worked as a marathon race versus a sprint. Helpers will *burn out* if they do not pace themselves. As people see the consistency of the ministry, more individuals will come for help. "If properly developed, it is my perhaps optimistic but I think realistic hope that every counseling need (except ones which involve organic problems) would be met within the church community."[22]

Summary

There are many risks hidden *behind our Sunday smiles,* including various kinds of life-controlling problems that will eventually destroy relationships with God and others. This ministry must come in the front door of the church and be viewed as available for everyone. People should not be labeled as addicts or some other description that may cause them to feel isolated from the congregation. Labels may cause people to feel inferior or contribute to a sense of hopelessness. Gary Sweeten in his work on the eight core conditions of helping states:

One of the keys to healing mental illness is to not label persons with diagnostic labels. A World Health Organization study found that in those countries that placed such labels on persons struggling with emotional stability, the recidivism rate (getting sick again) was much higher than in those countries where people were not labeled.[23]

Although labels can be valuable to summarize information, we should be careful not to judge or limit people with labels. Pinning labels on people may contribute to the segregation of the body of Christ or pride in the problem: "I am chemically dependent and no one in this church can help me." Labels, such as "midlife crisis," and "youth must go through a rebellious stage" [he must sow his wild oats] are often used to excuse or enforce negative behaviors.

Having a *sincere smile* or seemingly *having it together* does not mean a person is not struggling with a life-controlling problem. Ministry to these people and those who are in obvious pain or sorrow is Jesus at work. Matthew records the words of Jesus:

> When did we see you a stranger and invite you in, or needing clothes and clothed you? When did we see you sick or in prison and go to visit you? The King will reply, "I tell you the truth, whatever you did for one of the least of these brothers of mine, you did for me" (Matt. 25:38, 40).

One of my greatest privileges in Christian work during the last several years has been a friendship with Hugh O. Maclellan, Sr., the chairman of the Maclellan Foundation based in Chattanooga, Tennessee. He is one of the great Christian encouragers in America, although much of his work is behind the scenes. The Maclellan Foundation supports numerous Christian programs in the USA as well as internationally. The foundation places an emphasis mainly on the education and training of Christian young people in America along with a focus on Christian leadership training overseas. The group is vitally interested in evangelism at home and abroad.

I approached Mr. Maclellan in early 1981 to discuss the need for an ongoing drug prevention program in junior and senior high schools. Having been involved with Teen Challenge (a Christian growth program for people with life-controlling problems), I was keenly aware of the devastation caused by alcohol and other drugs among our young people. As a director with the Teen Challenge ministry I frequently spoke in high school assemblies and in classroom discussions. It was common for young people to talk with me after presentations and discuss (with tears in their eyes) their drug use which was unknown to their parents. Teachers would also respond to the presentations by saying, "The students are interested in what you said about drug prevention and intervention, but the concern will not last. They need this kind of assistance every day." After discussing this need with Mr. Maclellan, he suggested that I consult with certain key people and develop a plan for an ongoing drug prevention/intervention program for secondary schools.

Having a deep love for young people, Mr. Maclellan placed his support behind the planned pilot project in a Chattanooga-area high school in the fall of 1981. This approach, with a goal of reversing negative peer pressure, was named Project 714. Recognizing a need for healing in our land, this name came from 2 Chronicles 7:14.

With almost a school year's experience with Project 714, Mr. Maclellan, his son, Hugh Maclellan, Jr., and I met to discuss whether or not the project should continue into the next school year with two additional schools. We had observed some success in the first year; however, there were still several questions and the program was unproven. It was inspiring to me to observe this father and son's teamwork in planning the possible future of 714. I was aware of the terrible, growing drug problem among young people as were this father and son. However, I did not have the vision to the extent of my Christian brothers.

In our conversation I began to point out the various legal, financial, and personal risks that may be associated with expanding this unproven program for students. Mr. Maclellan, who is a very gentle person with firm convictions, asked me a question that I will not soon forget. He asked, "What are the risks if we choose to do nothing?" With this challenge 714 moved forward from the first school with 147 students being served to the present ongoing support of over 50,000 students in 55 school system in 10 states. (Project 714 is now known as STARS-Students Taking A Right Stand). We learned, with Mr. Maclellan's encouragement, that trained and loving teachers in our public schools could be very effective in addressing the issues of substance abuse.

With vision people in the local church (clerks, stock-exchange brokers, housewives, mechanics, teachers, and so forth) can be effective in helping each other deal with the various stages of life-controlling problems. Vision makes the difference. People with vision are willing to take a risk to help others. America has become an addictive society plagued by drug abuse, child abuse, abortions, and dysfunctional families. This certainly seems like risky work for the local church; however, the greatest risk may be "if we choose to do nothing."

Local Church Funnel

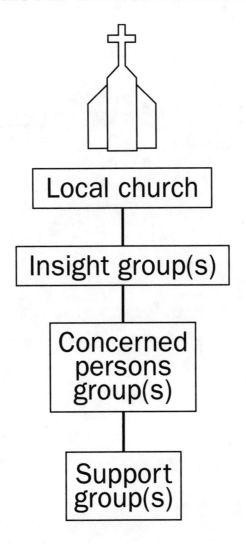

Insight Group Outline

1. **One Session Per Week** (approximately 75 minutes)

2. **Format**
   A. Introduction   (10 minutes)
   B. Self-awareness   (20 minutes)
   C. Spiritual awareness   (20 minutes)
   D. Spiritual application   (25 minutes)

3. **Course Outline**
   Session 1

Self-awareness	Orientation	
Spiritual awareness	Goals for course	2 Peter 1:3–11

   Session 2

Self-awareness	Trust	
Spiritual awareness	Faith	2 Peter 1:3–11

   Session 3

Self-awareness	The trap	
Spiritual awareness	Goodness	2 Peter 1:3–11

   Session 4

Self-awareness	Feelings	
Spiritual awareness	Knowledge	2 Peter 1:3–11

Session 5
Self-awareness   Defenses
Spiritual awareness   Self-control   2 Peter 1:3–11

Session 6
Self-awareness   Symptoms
Spiritual awareness   Perseverance   2 Peter 1:3–11

Session 7
Self-awareness   Peer evaluation
Spiritual awareness   Godliness   2 Peter 1:3–11

Session 8
Self-awareness   Peer evaluation
Spiritual awareness   Brotherly kindness   2 Peter 1:3–11

Session 9
Self-awareness   Peer evaluation
Spiritual awareness   Christian love   2 Peter 1:3–11

....

Concerned Persons Group Outline

1. **One Session Per Week** (approximately 75 minutes)

2. **Format**
   A.   Introduction   (10 minutes)
   B.   Self-awareness   (20 minutes)
   C.   Spiritual awarenes   (20 minutes)
   D.   Spiritual application   (25 minutes)

3. **Course Outline**
   Session 1
   Self-awareness   Orientation
   Spiritual awareness   Comfort   2 Corinthians 1:3-7

   Session 2
   Self-awareness   Hope
   Spiritual awareness   Apostle Paul and hope 2 Corinthians 1:7-11

   Session 3
   Self-awareness   Codependency
   Spiritual awareness   Serving the Creator   Romans 1:25

   Session 4
   Self-awareness   Feelings and defenses
   Spiritual awareness   Jesus and our feelings Hebrews 4:15

Session 5
Self-awareness   Letting go and letting
                           God
Spiritual awareness   Powerlessness   Romans 7:18, 24,
                                                           25

Session 6
Self-awareness   Care-fronting
Spiritual awareness   Jesus and care-
                           fronting   John 8:3-11

Session 7
Self-awareness   Peer evaluation
Spiritual awareness   Emotional healing   James 5:13-20

Session 8
Self-awareness   Peer evaluation
Spiritual awareness   Apostle Paul and
                           setting goals   Philippians 3:12-14

Session 9
Self-awareness   Peer evaluation
Spiritual awareness   Apostle Paul and a
                           new way of thinking   Ephesians 4:22-27

．．．

Twelve Steps of Wholeness

Following a tradition of the early church and the Wesley revival, the Oxford Group systematized a series of "steps" as a process of cleansing one's inner life. These "steps" were later adapted by Alcoholics Anonymous, with much of the Christian basis ignored. They are here re-adapted emphasizing this great Christian base so integral to the wholeness sought. Here the center of wholeness is recognized as the Lord Jesus Christ. The "steps" have also been changed to conform to other principles of discipleship and Christian growth. If a Christian will vigorously apply these principles, and make these decisions, that person will move toward "Teleios"—Wholeness in Christ.

1. I now see that I, of myself, am powerless, unable to control (manage) my life by myself.
    Romans 7–8   Romans 7:18–19   Psalm 32:3–7
                      Romans 3:9–10, 23

2. I now realize that my Creator, God the Father, Son, and Holy Spirit, can restore me to wholeness in Christ.
    Psalm 27:4–5   Mark 10:26–27   Philippians 2:13
    Romans 8:9   Ezekiel 36:27

3. I now make a conscious decision to turn my entire will and life over to the care and direction of Jesus Christ as Teacher, Healer, Savior, and Lord.
    Joshua 1:8–9   Jeremiah 29:11–14   Jeremiah 32:27
    John 14:6   John 10:30   Mark 10:27
                      Matthew 28:18, 20b

4. Having made this decision, I now obey God's call in Scripture to make a fearless, ethical, moral, and scriptural inventory of my entire life in order to uncover all sins, mistakes, and character defects, and to make a written list of every item uncovered.
    Psalm 139:23–24   Lamentations 3:40   Jeremiah 23:24
                           Romans 8:26-27

5. After completing this inventory I now will to "walk in the light, as he is in the light" by admitting to myself, to God, and to at least one other person in Christ the exact nature of these wrongs.
    I John 1:7   Ephesians 5:13–14   Psalm 119:9–11
    1 Timothy 1:15   Acts 13:38–39   James 5:13–16
    Hebrews 9:14   Acts 2:37–38

6. Having agreed with God about my sinful behavior, I now ask his forgiveness through Christ and openly acknowledge that I am forgiven according to the Scripture.
    1 John 1:8–9   James 4:10   1 John 2:1–2
    Psalm 27:13–14   Psalm 118:18, then 17

7. I now repent (turn away) from all these behaviors in thought, word, and deed, and ask God to remove each besetting sin, through Jesus Christ.
    John 5:14   John 8:10–11   Job 11:13–19
    Ezekiel 18:30–32   Romans 5, 6   Romans 12:1–2
    1 John 2:3–6   2 Corinthians 10:5
                           Colossians 3:17

8. I now make a list of all persons I have harmed in thought, word and deed, and a list of all persons I believe have harmed me, and will to make amends to all of them.
    Ephesians 4:29–32   Hosea 11:1–4   Ephesians 5:1–2
    Luke 6:31   Matthew 5:43–44   Matthew 18:15
    Leviticus 19:17–18   Mark 12:31   Matthew 5:9

9. I now go directly to these persons to forgive and to seek forgiveness, reconciliation, restitution, or release whenever and with whomever possible, unless to do so would cause further harm.
    Matthew 5:23–24   Isaiah 1:18–20

10. I now consciously and prayerfully continue to "walk in the light" by unceasingly taking personal inventory of all my temptations and sins, and by keeping a constantly open relationship with God, myself, and other persons.

Matthew 26:41	James 1:13–15	Matthew 6:11–13
Colossians 3:13	Proverbs 30:8–9	Ephesians 5:15–18
Psalm 4:3–5	Psalm 55:22	1 Peter 5:6–7
	Ephesians 4:22–28	

11. I now continue in regular Scripture, study, prayer, worship, and fellowship to increase God's will in my life.

Acts 2:42	Mark 12:28–33	Matthew 6:33
Psalm 89:15	Joshua 1:8	1 Kings 8:56–61
	Colossians 3:12–17	

12. Recognizing the impact of God in my life, I now intentionally share these principles and their effect with others as God's Spirit leads, and will to practice these principles in all areas of my life.

Micah 6:8	Ephesians 5:8	Psalm 40:8–10
Galatians 5:1	Revelation 12:11	2 Corinthians 3:17
	Ephesians 6:10–18	

Prepared by Dr. Gary R. Sweeten & Hall B. Schell

Published by permission of:
Equipping Ministries International
4015 Executive Park Drive Suite 309
Cincinnati, OH 45241

Small Groups Flow Chart

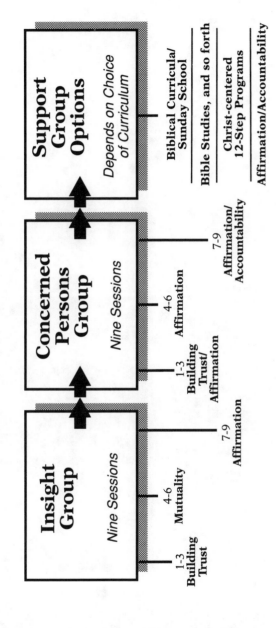

Insight Group

Nine Sessions

1-3
Building
Trust

4-6
Mutuality

7-9
Affirmation

Concerned Persons Group

Nine Sessions

1-3
Building
Trust/
Affirmation

4-6
Affirmation

7-9
Affirmation/
Accountability

Support Group Options

Depends on Choice of Curriculum

Biblical Curricula/ Sunday School

Bible Studies, and so forth

Christ-centered 12-Step Programs

Affirmation/Accountability

149

···

Dramatization of Life-Controlling Problems

Based on True Stories

Published by permission of : Turning Point Ministries, Inc.,
P.O. Box 8936, Chattanooga, TN 37411

Prepared by J. David Schmidt & Associates (708) 682-1990 for Turning Point Ministries

1. Susan's Story: Teenage Alcoholism

BILL: Don't make excuses for her this time, Martha. When Susan gets home, we're going to get to the bottom of this.

MARTHA: Please . . . Bill. This change has been difficult on her.

BILL: *No, Martha*! No more chances. Ever since we moved here, she's been pushing all the wrong buttons. Staying out half the night. Sleeping late. Skipping school. She won't even go to church anymore

without World War III breaking out. This is not our Susan.
Something's wrong.

MARTHA: She's seventeen—she's trying to find herself.

BILL: That's a pretty thin excuse, Martha. If she needs to find out
who she is have her come to me. I'll tell her who she is. She's my
daughter—and daughters raised in the church don't put their parents
through this! (*Pause.*) Shh . . . listen . . . there she is now.

SUSAN: Mom . . . Dad! (*Slurring.*) Howyadoin? Wow! . . . it's
late.Whaddya stayin so late up for? I mean . . . stayin' up so late for?

BILL: Oh, Lord, she's been drinking.

MARTHA: (*Under breath.*) Dear Jesus . . . help us.

BILL: I can't believe you're doing this, Susan!

SUSAN: (*Giggle.*) Don' start in on me, Daddy . . . I was just havin' little fun.

BILL: For goodness sake, Susan, do you think this is funny! Do you
see me laughing? You're drunk! And probably so were those . . . losers
you hang out with!

MARTHA: Bill!

SUSAN: Don' you call them losers . . . they're my friends. At least
they like me. . . .

BILL: (*Ignoring.*) That's it, young lady! From now on, you're
grounded. You are not seeing those people. Not going out at night for
three months. And you are to never drink again! *Do you understand*?

SUSAN: I won't do what you say! I won't!

BILL: (*Anger building.*) Oh, yes, you will. . . !

(*PAUSE.*)

SUSAN: (*Screaming.*) I won't. I'm old enough to make my own
disions . . . uh. . . decisions. You can't make me! You can go to. . .

BILL: (*Desperate.*) That's it! If I have to listen to any more of this,
I'm going to hit her! You deal with her. She's your daughter too, you
know.

Next Day

MARTHA: (*Pleading.*) Susan . . . Susan . . . why are you doing this, sweetheart? Why did last night happen? Why did you come in like that? You're only hurting yourself *and* us. What's going on here with this drinking?

SUSAN: Oh Mama . . . Mama . . . I don't have a problem. This is really only the first time I drank that much that it caused a problem.

Overview:

Normally life-controlling problems develop through predictable steps. The Bible says: "But each one is tempted when, by his own evil desire, he is dragged away and enticed. Then, after desire has conceived, it gives birth to sin; and sin, when it is full-grown, gives birth to death" (James 1:14–15)

People with life-controlling problems become unfeeling. But Jesus sympathizes with us even when our feelings are numb. The Bible also says:

> Therefore, since we have a great high priest who has gone through the heavens, Jesus the Son of God, let us hold firmly to the faith we profess. For we do not have a high priest who is unable to sympathize with our weaknesses, but we have one who has been tempted in every way, just as we are—yet was without sin. Let us then approach the throne of grace with confidence, so that we may receive mercy and find grace to help us in our time of need (Heb. 4:14–16)

2. Joe's Story: Sexual Addiction

Note: Throughout this story we will hear two voices: Joe and his cravings.

JOE 1: (*Talking to self.*) Ah . . . this blasted traffic. C'mon light— change! Isn't that typical? I get out of work an hour early only to hit more traffic. (*Sighs.*) Wonder what Linda's got on the stove tonight— leftovers again, I suppose.

JOE'S C: (*Sarcastic.*) Another big night in store for you, Joey boy!

JOE 1: Yeah . . . great. We'll sit and watch one dumb show after another, and she'll end up in bed early. Some romantic marriage this is turning out to be. I could go for some passion. I'll probably end up getting an earful about the kids' day in school or her aches and pains. I can't remember the last time she and I . . .

JOE's C: (*Interrupts self.*) Hey, hey, hey! Where did *she* come from? Nice legs. I'll just spin into the parking lot and get a little closer look. Boy, she sure knows how to dress.

JOE 1: (*Sighs.*) C'mon, Joe. Clean it up. Don't let yourself do this again.

JOE's C: (*Pauses.*) Wait a minute . . . why not!? Linda won't ever know. Besides, she's not what she used to be. You think Linda's going to be waiting at home? Huh! Fat chance! She's never done that kind of thing for me like other women do for their husbands. That's right . . . for me! I have needs, too, you know.

JOE 1: (*Pauses, sarcastic.*) Great! Another red light—and there's the Bachelor's Library and Club.

JOE's C: Looks pretty empty tonight. Little chance of being spotted if I drive around back.

JOE 1: What are you doing, Joe?

JOE's C: Yeah. Let's go!

JOE 1: Are you really going to do this again, Joe?

JOE's C: (*Pauses.*) You bet I am! And why shouldn't I? It's not like it's adultery or anything. Heck! I even read somewhere that half the church leaders in this country look at pornography. Every man does—right: I mean . . . it's the way we're made. We're attracted by what we see. It's not like I'm going to get involved with her or become a sex addict. Anyway, it takes my mind off my problems. Just a few minutes this time.

JOE 1: Joe.

JOE's C: One quick show and maybe a new magazine this trip. Yeah.

JOE 1: Joe.

JOE's C: Satisfy myself and then go home. I've been cutting back on these visits so I deserve it.

JOE 1: Joe. (*Defeated.*) I can't believe it. Joe, you idiot! Why did you do this again? Real brilliant. For a few minutes of thrills looking at some woman who could care less about you, you're going to put your reputation—and your family's on the line? Where's it gonna end, Joey boy!? How many peep shows and magazines are you going to buy? Hire yourself a prostitute, next time? Get caught? End up with your name in the paper?

JOE 1: (*Grunts angrily at self.*) Shut up! Why can't I stop this? Why does God seem so far away? Lord . . . help me stop next time. Help me stop. Next Friday's our anniversary. I'll stop then.

Overview:

Our thought life needs direction or it will lead us into unhealthy compromises. Direction begins with renewing our mind through the Word. A renewed mind yields right thinking. Right thinking generates right behavior. Finally, right behavior results in right feelings. The Bible says:

> For everything in the world—the cravings of sinful man, the lust of his eyes and the boasting of what he has and does—comes not from the Father but from the world. The world and its desires pass away, but the man who does the will of God lives forever (1 John 2:16, 17).

3. Gary's Story: Delusion Over Drug Dependency

THERESA: (*Calling.*) Gary! You're going to be late again! C'mon, get up.

(*In the background a child cries loudly.*)

THERESA: Peter, stop pulling your sister's hair!

GARY: (*Yawning.*) Sorry . . . I'm just so tired lately. What's the time?

THERESA: Quarter to—and I'm not calling in anymore making excuses for you—it's just not right. Why are you always so tired lately? I could use a little help in the mornings.

GARY: Ah . . . I need some coffee. (*Pauses.*) I've just had to put in so many hours . . . since the merger . . . you know.

THERESA: Gary! The merger was over a year ago. I just don't understand why you have to work so much. Most nights you don't come in till past nine. You don't even see the kids anymore.

GARY: Look . . . I told you . . . it's not going to be forever. I spend plenty of time with the kids.

THERESA: (*Incredulous.*) Are we talking about the same family here? Every weekend for the last two months you spend Saturday afternoons napping. Have you looked at the yard lately? We're going to get fined by the community association for all the weeds. And when was the last time you got up and went to church with us on Sundays?

GARY: (*Defensive.*) Look, Theresa. My job is why we've got a house like this and two cars and grocery money. Give me a break—all I'm doing is trying to pay the bills.

THERESA: Bills? Then why are we always bouncing checks? How come I always find these unexplained automatic teller transactions on the bank statement?

GARY: (*Growing angry.*) Look . . . how many times do I have to tell you about that? Since I got that promotion, they expect me to take clients out for lunch. I don't always get reimbursed.

(*A child cries again.*)

GARY: *Shut up, Lisa!* (*Child cries and keeps crying.*)

THERESA: Gary, you're not the same person you were a year ago. What's going on?

GARY: Nothing's going on. Just leave me alone!

THERESA: (*Soothing.*) It's all right, baby. Daddy didn't mean to scare you. It's going to be all right.

GARY: I'm changing. Gimme a break. (*Clinking in a bathroom.*) Who does she think she is? I'm not changing. Still the same old Gary. Yeah—same old Gary.
C'mon I know it's in here. Where is it? Where's my little friend? Oh . . . here it is . . . whew. Snowstorm in a little tin can. Okay . . . yeah (*Long sniff.*) This is all I need—a trip to the land of feeling good. Just a little recreational boost for the morning meeting. I can quit anytime I want. No problem. (*Pause.*) Just not today.

Overview:

Fooling ourselves that a problem doesn't exist only leads to a state of delusion. It is a downward spiral. The Bible says:

> The god of this age has blinded the minds of unbelievers, so that they cannot see the light of the gospel of the glory of Christ, who is the image of God (2 Cor. 4:4).

And in Ephesians:

> But everything exposed by the light becomes visible, for it is light that makes everything visible. This is why it is said:
>
> "Wake up, O sleeper,
>   rise from the dead,
>   and Christ will shine on you" (Ephesians 5:13, 14).

4. Linda's Story: Troubled Self-esteem

FATHER: Oh, Lord, we thank you for all the blessings of this past year. For your provision and kindness. Bless this Thanksgiving table to our nourishment and enjoyment. Amen. (*Pause.*) Let's eat, gang!

MOTHER: Linda, honey, how 'bout some sweet potatoes to go with your turkey and stuffing?

LINDA: Oh okay, Mama. But just a little.

MOTHER: What's wrong, aren't you feeling well, honey?

LINDA: I'm fine, Mama. Just trying to watch my weight for Homecoming next week.

FATHER: Watch your weight! Lord, sweetie, you're already thinner than thin. You look like a broomstick with arms. Don't they feed you at that college? Come on now—it's Thanksgiving!

LINDA: I know, but . . .

MOTHER: Now, Bob, don't push her.

FATHER: No, no, no . . . no excuses, now! I may not be able to watch over you everyday anymore, but when you're home from school, you're going to fly right and eat what you're served. Mother, fill up that girl's plate.

LINDA: (*Acquiescing.*) Okay, Daddy.

FATHER: Good. No daughter of mine is gonna shrivel up and blow away—not while I have anything to say about it. In fact, I'm going to write that dean of yours a letter about the lousy cafeteria food they must be feeding you at that school.

MOTHER: Linda, how do you like my new stuffing recipe? Isn't that good?

LINDA: (*Smacking lips, licking fingers.*) Oh, mother, yes. It really is. It's all so good. I don't know what I must have been thinking. After all—it's Thanksgiving! Daddy, pass me those yummy yams again—and the stuffing.

FATHER: You bet, kiddo. I just love it when we can be together again. Jason, how you doing down there? Need anything?
Yessir . . . this is one family that knows how to enjoy the holidays. I wanted to tell you kids about what they're talking about doing downtown. (*As father rambles on his voice fades to silence for a short pause.*)

LINDA: Go ahead, Dad. I need to be excused for a minute. I'll be right back.

LINDA: (*In the bathroom—coughing.*) Oh . . . dear Jesus . . . (*Heavy breathing—straining to catch breath.*)
Oh, God . . . I hate this but I've been looking so gross lately. I don't know though. I think I'm getting thinner. All I want is to be like the other girls in the dorm. They're all so beautiful—and thin. Jesus, why can't I lose weight faster? Why can't I get skinny? It's useless.

Overview:

Our self-worth is best communicated or reflected back to us by someone who is perfect. And that's God. Living at peace with him is critical to our self-esteem. The Bible says:

"You, my brothers, were called to be free. But do not use your freedom to indulge the sinful nature; rather, serve one another in love. The entire law is summed up in a single command: "Love your neighbor as yourself" (Gal. 5:13, 14).

Such confidence as this is ours through Christ before God. Not that we are competent in ourselves to claim anything for ourselves, but our competence comes from God (2 Cor. 3:4, 5).

5. Art's Story:
Enabling a Wife's Compulsion

Art: (*Answering ringing phone.*) Hello . . . (*Pauses.*) Carolyn . . . what's wrong, honey? Hold on . . . hold on . . . tell me where you are. (*Pauses.*) The police station! Oh . . . Carolyn not again! What was it this time? (*Pauses.*) And they're pressing charges? Yeah . . . well, we had to know they were going to do it sooner or later, didn't we? (*Pauses.*) All right . . . calm down. Get control of yourself. I'll get you out of this. You can count on me. (*Sighs.*) I'll be right down. (*Dials phone number.*)

Art: Mom? Hi. Could you run over here right away and watch the kids? Carolyn got caught shoplifting again. (*Pause.*) *Why* I married her is not the issue, Mom. (*Pause.*) Yeah, I know . . . I know . . . What I *don't* know is how I'm going to bail her out of this one. (*Pause.*) Why does she do this? I don't know. It's got to be something in her past that makes her steal things, I guess. (*Sighs.*)

And it's so stupid. It's always just worthless trinkets. It's not like we can't afford the stuff. She never tells me why—she *can't* tell me why. I know she was neglected, but she's an adult now. Why can't she stop this and grow up? (*Pauses.*) Maybe a new environment would help. Maybe it's just the pressures of this city. Maybe if we moved—or tried a new church, everything would be okay. I've got to fix this somehow. I just don't know. I'll see you in a bit. (*Hangs up.*)

Art: (*To himself.*) Sure, Art . . . go ahead . . . fool yourself. She's not changing. She can't change. And why? Because she likes it . . . this attention . . . doesn't she? I can't believe she would embarrass me this way! Everybody at church knows. I see the stares when we walk in on Sundays. Why is she doing this to me again? What would she think if I just up and divorced her? I bet she'd think twice about doing this then, wouldn't she? I can't even think straight anymore, Lord! You've got to get us out of this. . . just one more time. I promise . . . I'll find her some help . . . I really will. Just please change the hearts of those people at the store. Help them not to press charges. (*Pauses.*) Oh, I don't know. This just can't be that serious. It'll all work out in time. She's just going through a phase.

Overview:

It is possible to get in the way of God's work when we enable or rescue people from the natural consequences for their sin. Jezebel did it when she had Naboth killed so his vineyard could be obtained by her pouting husband Ahab. The Bible says:

Let us not become weary in doing good, for at the proper time we will reap a harvest if we do not give up. Therefore, as we have opportunity, let us do good to all people, especially to those who belong to the family of believers (Gal. 6:9, 10).

6. *"Terry's Story: Care-fronting an Alcoholic*

OFFICER: (*Gruffly*) Take your seat over there sir—at the third booth and pick up the phone. You can talk to your son through the glass that way. Ten minutes is all you got. Make it count.

FATHER: Hello, Son. Do you feel like talking?

TERRY: I already know what you're going to say, Dad. I messed up again, right? Let's tell the whole world: Terry Richards just got his third DUI in a year. Driving under the influence of alcohol. Whoa! Lucky he didn't hit a kid on a bicycle, right? Lucky he didn't maim an old lady. Yep. Good, old, dependable Terry. Tell you what—whatever it is—I've heard it before. So why don't you just save yourself the trouble and the breath.

FATHER: Actually, Terry, I do want to talk to you. But this time, no yelling, no screaming. No more lectures. You're an adult, son. You're twenty-one. The law says you can drink. Even if I wanted to, I couldn't lecture you on drinking now. Your mother and I just wanted to make sure you were okay—and have everything you need.

TERRY: (*Sarcastic.*) Oh, you bet, Dad. Every twenty-one-year-old is ready to be locked up with a bunch of homos and crazies. What I want to know is how you're going to get me out of here.

FATHER: Terry, I know we've had our run-ins. But I want you to know there's nothing you could ever do to make us stop loving you. It's just this time, son . . . I'm afraid, there's not much I can do. You know the law as well as I do: three DUIs is it—automatic jail time.

TERRY: Dad! That's not what I want to hear. You've always had a way out for me before. Isn't your attorney friend still around? What about some kind of home supervision thing? Come on. I can't believe you'd just leave me here.

FATHER: The truth is, son, we played all our cards last time.

TERRY: (*Voice breaking.*) Wake me up and tell me this is not happening.

FATHER: You don't know how I wish I could tell you that myself. But it's time for us to look at what we're facing here. I'd like to discuss an option with you you've probably already been thinking of, but I think it's important that we consider it again.

TERRY: Not rehab! No way! I've told you a million times. *I'm not an alcoholic!*

FATHER: That's not for me to judge, Terry. But the fact is the court will view you as an alcoholic. I feel they'll order you into a treatment program, whether you like it or not. With three DUIs and grades going down, Mom and I feel you need this kind of help. And the really good thing is, Terry, I feel *you'll* know for sure where *you stand.*

TERRY: You really think so?

FATHER: I do—but the important thing is: attitude. The judge will be able to tell if you're bluffing. I feel it's important that you search, really search yourself for some answers these next few days. (*Pause.*) Son, I feel you need to be brutally honest with yourself, about where you are right now. You know where your mother and I stand with God, and I just want you to know that he's there for you whenever you ask. But *you* have to ask. He won't force himself on you.

TERRY: Dad . . . I don't think Jesus can hear me anymore because of everything I've done.

FATHER: It's exactly everything you've done that makes Jesus so ready and willing to hear you right now.

OFFICER: Okay, Mr. Richards. Time's up.

FATHER: Just one more moment, officer. (*Pause.*) Terry, your mother and I are going to pray that God will give you clear thinking about your life—and the important choices you've got to make—and that you'll know above all that God loves you and wants to help you overcome this drinking problem.

OFFICER: Time's up.

FATHER: I love you, son.

Overview:

Care-fronting is the truth spoken or delivered in love. It is not protecting people from the truth or consequences of their behavior. The Bible says:

> Let your conversation be always full of grace, seasoned with salt, so that you may know how to answer everyone (Col. 4:6).

7. Chuck and Sally's Story: Dysfunctional Parenting

In a busy restaurant with soft piano music in background.

CHUCK: (*Loudly.*) Waiter . . . check, please! (*Pauses.*) I can't believe this, Sally. This was supposed to be *our* evening, and we end up talking about the kids all night! I'm getting real tired of this. When are we going to think about us for once? God knows we need to the way this marriage has gone!

SALLY: (*Offended, sarcastic.*) Well thank you, Mister Romance! You sure did your part to make it a romantic evening—getting home an hour and a half late. Rushing around. *No shower.* And besides, Chuck, we *need* to talk about the kids. They've been on my mind for several days, especially Julie—only you never want to talk when you get home!

CHUCK: They're always on your mind. As far as I'm concerned, there's no reason why Julie shouldn't have her own car.

SALLY: That wasn't what I meant, but since we're on that subject . . .

CHUCK: I don't know what you're so uptight about. Julie's got a good head on her shoulders. Remember, I had my own car when we were in high school.

SALLY: I remember the car. That's just what I'm worried about. She's only sixteen, and I just don't think a sixteen-year-old ought to have to deal with a heavy responsibility like that. I think there are some other things—besides a car—that we need to be helping her with right now.

CHUCK: Like what?

SALLY: Well . . . things . . . you know! Her personal development and rights as a young woman—and some decisions *she's* going to have to make. Sex. You know.

CHUCK: Sex! I don't like the way this conversation's heading. (*Louder, impatient.*) *Waiter*! Check!

SALLY: You may not like the way it's heading, Chuck, but we've got to open our eyes. Julie's not our baby girl anymore. She's a beautiful, young woman with a very strong will—in a very permissive world. We've been denying the realities too long. How are we supposed to teach her to say "no" when we never really deal with the topic openly *and* when everything else around her tells her to say "yes"?

CHUCK: Well, I sure can say *No!* and I just decided to say *No* to this car business! If you're worried about her and what she's doing on her dates, speak up. And I'll put the car right out of reach for her.

SALLY: You really think that will work with her now, Chuck? We've got a lot of ground to make up. I'll talk to her if you won't.

CHUCK: Thanks for the vote of confidence.

SALLY: That's not the point. But somebody's got to be in *charge* of this family. Listen, I heard about this family counseling program at the church when I was there on Sunday. I think maybe . . .

CHUCK: (*Interrupting.*) Hold it right there . . . I'm not listening to someone no better off than I am tell me how terrible a parent I am—and how Jesus is the simple answer for every problem. I don't want any part of it. Those people are all a bunch of hypocrites with their money-grubbing scandals—and God only knows what else they're into.

SALLY: Well, I personally think you're using a pretty broad brush to paint them with. But I'm afraid we're going to need some help sooner than you think.

CHUCK: (*Uneasy voice.*) What are you talking about?

SALLY: (*Pause.*) I found birth-control pills in Julie's room this morning.

Overview:

Parents have got to stand together in working with their kids. Submitting to each other and being a team *always* yields better results. The Bible says:

> Has not the LORD made them one? In flesh and spirit they are his. And why one? Because he was seeking godly offspring. So guard yourself in your spirit, and do not break faith with the wife of your youth (Mal. 2:15).

(Single parents are not necessarily dysfunctional. Handling authority and communication with children requires the same approach and wisdom required in a two-parent home.)

James 1:5 says: "If any of you lacks wisdom, he should ask God, who gives generously to all without finding fault, and it will be given to him."

8. Helen's Story: Codependency

Sound of footsteps going downstairs.

HELEN: (*In disgust*) Look at this. I wish that man would clean this place out. I can't believe it. What a pack rat. Come looking for a screwdriver and you have to wade through the world's biggest collection of junk, tools, old newspapers.

HELEN: I tell you . . . What's he got in *this* old thing? (*Pauses*) C'mon Helen. Turn around. Forget about the box. What you don't know *can't* hurt you, right? That's the rule around here. If you don't want to know—don't ask. I just wonder though . . .

HELEN: (*Gasp.*) I knew it! (*Pause.*) Where does he buy this stuff? I can't believe this! It's a stash. It's a whole box full of smut! I thought we were through with all that. He promised me! He told me he wouldn't do this anymore! August '87—June '86. He's been keeping this stuff for years! Lord, why didn't he keep his promise?

HELEN: It's probably no big deal (*Under her breath.*). But he promised!

TRICIA: (*Voice in distance.*) Helen? Are you down there?

HELEN: I don't think it's a problem. He has a good reason for this. But, *he promised*!

(*Another bang, this time smashing a bottle.*)

HELEN: (*Breaking into sobs.*) Lord, get me out of this trap. He promised—*he promised*. Lord, what do I . . .?

TRICIA: Helen . . . are you okay?

HELEN: (*Recovering.*) Tricia . . . uh . . . I didn't hear you come in upstairs. Yeah, I'm okay. (*Helen recovers.*).

TRICIA: I was just dropping by some blueberries and I heard this smash. Is everything okay?

HELEN: (*Covering.*) Uh . . . yes . . . sorry. Bumped into the workbench and knocked over a bottle of cleaning fluid. Hard to imagine doing that in this orderly place right? (*A forced laugh.*)

TRICIA: Yeah . . . I see what you mean. Aren't all men alike? I have the same problem with Bart. I can't get him off the couch to clean up our basement either. (*Pause.*) Say . . . how's everything going with you and Jerry?

HELEN: Except for this basement . . . couldn't be better. . . it just seems to be getting better and better.

Overview:

Sin has a way of impacting more than just the person committing it. When it touches others who care, it can distract that person from focusing on Christ and war against their sense of well-being. This is codependency. The Bible says:

Let us fix our eyes on Jesus, the author and perfecter of our faith, who for the joy set before him endured the cross, scorning its shame, and sat down at the right hand of the throne of God (Heb. 12:2).

Resources, National Organizations

Alcoholics for Christ
1316 North Campbell Road
Royal Oak, MI 48067
1-800-441-7877

National Teen Challenge
1525 N. Campbell Avenue
Springfield, MO 65803
417-862-6969

National Clearinghouse for
Alcohol Information
P.O. Box 1908
Rockville, MD 20850
301-468-2600

National Institute of Alcohol,
Alcohol Abuse, Drug Abuse &
Mental Health
5600 Fishers Lane
Rockville, MD 20857
301-443-2403

Turning Point Ministries, Inc.
P.O. Box 8936
Chattanooga, TN 37411
615-899-4770

Overcomers Outreach, Inc.
2290 West Whittier Boulevard
LaHabra, CA 90631
213-697-3994

STARS-Students Taking A Right
Stand
A Program of Project 714, Inc.
P.O. Box 8936
Chattanooga, TN 37411
1-800-476-0714

Community Intervention
529 South Seventh Street
Suite 570
Minneapolis, MN 55415
1-800-328-0417

Liontamers
2801 North Brea Blvd.
Fullerton, CA 92635-2799
1-714-529-5544

Resources for Small Group Bible Studies

Challenge Bible Study Series (Baker Book House, P. O. Box 6287, Grand Rapids, MI 49516-6287 [616-676-9185])

This new series has been designed for Christians who are acquainted with the Bible but desire some meaningful materials to continue study and growth. Each book has thirteen chapters, appropriate for a one-quarter Sunday school class or neighborhood group. Leaders may use questions and content for a stimulating Bible study or may go on to develop their own material.

The Christian Business Men's Committee of USA (1800 McCallie Avenue, Chattanooga, TN 37404)

This is an international organization of evangelical Christian business and professional men whose primary purpose is to present Jesus Christ as Savior and Lord to other business and professional men and to train these men to carry out the Great Commission. CBMC publishes a number of materials geared to evangelism and discipleship, including *First Steps* (a four-part basic Bible study); *Operation Timothy* (a twelve-concept, one-to-one discipleship program); and *Living Proof* (a small group video series that trains Christians in the process and principles of lifestyle evangelism).

Equipping Ministries International (4015 Executive Park Drive, Suite 309, Cincinnati, OH 45241 [513-769-5353])

These materials are designed to help pastors and ministers of pastoral care who need a systematic way to equip the laity in the skills of lay pastoring, lay counseling, deaconing, hospital visitation, missing and marginal member recovery, and so forth.

Fisherman Bible Study Guides (Harold Shaw Publishers, P. O. Box 567, Wheaton IL 60189 [708-665-6700])

These are inductive studies for use by neighborhood, student, and church groups. Titles are arranged according to the following categories: (1) core studies; (2) Bible book studies; and (3) topical studies. Other series available: Young Fisherman Bible Study Guides (for teens) and Network Discussion Guide.

The Group Studies for New Christians (National Teen Challenge, 1525 N. Campbell Avenue, Springfield, MO 65803 [417-862-6969])

These studies include fourteen courses to introduce basic Christian living skills and appeal especially to Christians interested in spiritual growth. Special emphasis helps students begin to apply these teachings in their daily living. These courses can easily be used in a Christian support group or a Sunday school class. Both teacher and student materials are available. Subjects include: attitude, anger, failure, obedience to God and man, temptation, personal relationships with others, and more.

The Healthy Christian Life by Frank Minirth et al. (Grand Rapids: Baker Book House, 1988)

Included are sixty-three Bible study units that present a comprehensive and healthy approach to Christian living. The studies are theologically and psychologically sound and offer a positive approach. The variety of topics covered range from the basic Christian lifestyle to common emotional problems. Each unit features Scripture for individual study, a personal project, and additional enrichment assignments.

How to Start a Neighborhood Bible Study by Marilyn Kunz and Catherine Schell (Neighborhood Bible Studies, Box 222, Dobbs Ferry, NY 10522 [914-693-3273])

The guides provide discussion questions to lead a group through careful, inductive Bible study. Guides are available for many of the books of the Bible, in addition to a series on New Testament characters and one on basic Christian doctrines.

Insight for Living, publishers of study guides by Charles Swindoll, P. O. Box 4444, Fullerton, CA 92634 [714-870-9161])

The study guides are based on Swindoll's sermon notes and the transcripts of his sermons.

Life Application Bible Studies (Tyndale House, P. O. Box 80, Wheaton, IL 60189 [800-323-9400])

Based on the Life Application Bible, this Bible study series offers several helpful features: the complete text of the book being studied contained in the guide; carefully grouped discussion questions; easy-to-understand study notes covering background, history, geography, and culture; application notes to help group members put into practice what they've learned; and charts, maps, and profiles of Bible people that present biblical truths in unique and helpful way. These ready-to-use lessons stimulate thought, discussion, and practical application.

The Life Change Series (NavPress, P. O. Box 6000, Colorado Springs, CO 80934 [800-366-7788])

Life change Bible studies offer the joy of firsthand discovery while emphasizing personal application. Ideal for individual or small group studies The Life Change series has become a best-seller among Christians who study the Bible.

The Lifeguide Bible Study Series (InterVarsity Press, Box 1400, Downers Grove, IL 60515 [708-964-5700])

The goal of this series is to help group members "be guided by God's Word in every area of life." Thought provoking and personal, these inductive studies expose group members to promises, assurances, exhortations, and challenges of God's Word. The series is divided into three areas of study: topical (including "Christian Character," "Marriage," and "Spiritual Gifts"); Old Testament books (including Genesis, Exodus, and Psalms); and New Testament books (including Matthew, James, and Revelation).

Precept Bible Studies by Kay Arthur (Precept Ministries, P. O. Box 182218, Chattanooga, TN 37422 [615-892-6814])

Inductive Bible study courses for those who want the meat of the Word of God.

Radiant Life Elective Series (Gospel Publishing House, 1445 Boonville Avenue, Springfield, MO 65802 [800-641-4310])

Over forty different courses that deal with family life, Bible study, doctrine, Christian living, witnessing, and so forth.

Serendipity (Box 1012, Littleton, CO 80160 [800-525-9563])

Serendipity seminars led by Lyman Coleman are offered nation-wide. Materials include: Lifestyle Small Group Series, The Group Bible Study Series, Mastering the Basics Series, Youth Bible Studies,

Support Group Series, Serendipity Bible for Groups, and The
Serendipity New Testament.

The Twelve Steps—A Spiritual Journey (Recovery Publications,
1201 Knoxville Street, San Diego, CA 92110 [619-275-1350])
This is a comprehensive working guide based on biblical teachings
for adult children from addictive and other dysfunctional families.

Resources for Leaders of Small Groups

Cho, Paul Yonggi, *Successful Home Cell Groups*. Plainfield, NJ: Logos
International, 1981.

Griffin, Em. *Getting Together: A Guide for Good Groups*. Downers
Grove, IL: InterVarsity Press, 1982.

Hadaway, Kirk C., Stuart A. Wright, and Francis M. Dubose. *Home
Cell Groups and House Churches*. Nashville: Broadman Press, 1987.

Hestenes, Roberta. *Building Christian Community Through Small
Groups* (cassette audio-tape package). Fuller Seminary Media
Services Department, Fuller Seminary, Pasadena, CA 91182. This
kit includes taped lectures, *Using the Bible in Groups*, and an
expanded course syllabus.

_____. *Using the Bible in Groups*. Philadelphia, PA: Westminster
Press, 1985.

Hunt, Gladys. *You Can Start a Bible Study*. Wheaton, IL: Harold Shaw
Publishers, 1984.

Navigators. *How to Lead Small Group Bible Studies*. Colorado Springs,
CO: NavPress, 1982.

Nichols, Ron et al. *Good Things Come in Small Groups*. Downers
Grove, IL: InterVarsity Press, 1982.

_____. *Small Group Leader's Handbook*. Downers Grove, IL:
InterVarsity Press, 1982.

Peace, Richard. *Small Group Evangelism*. Downers Grove, IL:
InterVarsity Press, 1985.

Richards, Lawrence. *A New Face for the Church* (1981); *69 Ways to
Start a Study Group* (2d ed., 1980); *A Theology of Christian
Education* (1975). Grand Rapids: Zondervan Publishing Company.

Snyder, Howard. *The Problem of Wineskins*. Downers Grove, IL:
InterVarsity Press, 1975.

Notes

Chapter 1: Introduction to Life-Controlling Problems

1. Gerald G. May, M.D., *Addiction and Grace* (San Francisco: Harper & Row, 1988), 14.

2. Charles F. Stanley, *Handle with Prayer* (Wheaton: Victor Books, 1982), 118.

3. Patricia O'Gorman, Philip Oliver-Diaz, *Breaking the Cycle of Addiction* (Deerfield Beach: Health Communications, 1987), 128.

4. Jeffrey VanVonderen, *Good News for the Chemically Dependent* (Nashville: Thomas Nelson, 1985), 16.

5. Frank Minirth, Paul Meier, Siegfried Fink, Walter Byrd, Don Hawkins, *Taking Control* (Grand Rapids: Baker Book House, 1988), 54.

6. Ibid., 57–58.

7. Patrick Carnes, *Out of the Shadows: Understanding Sexual Addiction* (Minneapolis: CompCare Publishers, 1985), 13.

8. Joseph A. Muldoon, *Insight Class Program* (Minneapolis: Community Intervention, 1987), 75.

9. Vernon E. Johnson, *I'll Quit Tomorrow* (San Francisco: Harper and Row Publishers, 1980), 8.

10. Carnes, *Out of the Shadows*, 9.

11. O'Gorman, *Cycle of Addiction*, 35.

12. J. Keith Miller, *Sin—Overcoming the Ultimate Deadly Addiction* (San Francisco: Harper & Row, 1987), 95.

13. Jim Holwerda and David Egner, "Doing Away with Addiction," *Discovery Digest* 12:4 (1988), 7, 8.

14. VanVonderen, *Good News for Chemically Dependent*, 97.

15. Stanley, *Handle with Prayer*, 118.

16. Johnson, *I'll Quit Tomorrow*, 135.

17. Ibid., 132.

18. Miller, *Overcoming the Ultimate Addiction*, 101.

19. Stanley M. Horton, *What the Bible Says About the Holy Spirit* (Springfield, MO: Gospel, 1976), 228, 229.

Chapter 2: Ways to Help Hurting People

1. Jimmy Lee, *Turning Point Instructors Guide* (Chattanooga: Project 714, 1988), 47.
2. David G. Benner, ed., *Psychotherapy in Christian Perspective* (Grand Rapids: Baker Book House, 1987), 88, 89.
3. Lawrence J. Crabb, Jr., *Effective Biblical Counseling* (Grand Rapids: Zondervan Publishing House, 1977), 163.
4. Detailed descriptions of the Eight Core Conditions of Helping are shown in Gary Sweeten, *Apples of Gold I and II* (Cincinnati: Christian Information Committee, 1983).
5. Benner, *Psychotherapy in Christian Perspective*, 89.
6. Gary R. Collins, *Christian Counseling* (Waco: Word, 1980), 25.
7. David A. Seamands, *Healing for Damaged Emotions* (Wheaton: Victor Books, 1981), 139.
8. Gary Sweeten, *Apples of Gold II*, 66.
9. Melody Beattie, *Codependent No More* (New York: Harper & Row, 1988), 78.
10. VanVonderen, *Good News for the Chemically Dependent*, 158.
11. Detailed descriptions of the five-step process that dying people experience are shown in Elizabeth Kübler-Ross, *On Death and Dying* (New York: Macmillan Publishing Co., 1970).
12. Beattie, *Codependent No More*, 124,125.
13. Archibald D. Hart, *Counseling the Depressed* (Dallas: Word, 1987), 48.
14. Holwerda and Egner, *Doing Away with Addiction*, 7.
15. Detailed descriptions of ways to care-front are shown in David Augsburger, *Caring Enough to Confront* (Glendale: Regal Books, 1980).
16. Ibid., 20.
17. Johnson, *I'll Quit Tomorrow*, 136.
18. Detailed descriptions of how to conduct a guided intervention are shown in Louis B. and Elizabeth Krupnick, *From Despair to Decision* (Minneapolis: CompCare Publishers, 1985).

Chapter 3: Helping Families with Dependencies

1. Ralph G. Turnbull, ed., *Baker's Handbook of Practical Theology*, (Grand Rapids: Baker Book House, 1967), 221.
2. Minirth, *Taking Control*, 60, 61.
3. Collins, *Christian Counseling*, 455.
4. Beattie, *Codependent No More*, 31.
5. Detailed descriptions of codependent relationships are shown

in Kathy Capell-Sowder, *Codependency: An Emerging Issue*, (Pompano Beach: Health Communications, 1984).

6. Capel-Sowder, *Codependency: An Emerging Issue*, 22, 23.

7. Collins, *Christian Counseling*, 206.

8. O'Gorman, *Cycle of Addiction*, 112.

9. Charles Leerhsen and Tessa Namuth "Alcohol and the Family," *Newsweek* CXI (18 January 1988): 63.

10. Ibid., 67.

Chapter 4: A Local Church Model

1. VanVonderen, *Good News for Chemically Dependent*, 13, 14.

2. Minirth, *Taking Control*, 123.

3. Nills G. Friberg, "Health-Giving Church Communities: Biblical Sources and Practical Implications," Paper presented at the International Congress on Christian Counseling, Atlanta, Georgia, 7–13 November 1988.

4. Minirth, *Taking Control*, 147–148.

5. Miller, *Sin, 207.*

6. Roberta Hestenes, *Using the Bible in Groups*, (Philadelphia: The Westminister Press, 1985), 10.

7. Benner, *Psychotherapy in Christian Perspective*, 319.

8. H. Newton Malony, Thomas L. Needham, Samuel Southard, *Clergy Malpractice* (Philadelphia: The Westminister Press, 1986), 113.

9. S. Bruce Narramore, *No Condemnation* (Grand Rapids: Zondervan Publishing Co., 1984), 33.

10. Stephen P. Apthorp, *Alcohol and Substance Abuse* (Wilton, CT: Morehouse-Barlow, 1985), 33.

11. Bob Parker, *Small Groups: Workable Wineskins* (Cincinnati: Christian Information Committee, 1988), 27.

12. Hestenes, *Using the Bible in Groups*, 31.

13. C. Kirk Hadaway, Stuart A. Wright and Francis M. DuBose, *Home Cell Groups and House Churches* (Nashville: Broadman Press, 1987), 11.

14. Miller, *Sin,* 23.

15. Minirth, *Taking Control*, 147.

16. Apthorp, *Alcohol and Substance Abuse*, 32, 33.

17. Minirth, *Taking Control*, 97.

18. Hestenes, *Using the Bible in Groups*, 34.

19. Stanley, *Handle with Prayer*, 120.

20. Malony, *Clergy Malpractice*, 111.

21. Ibid., 106.

22. Crall, *Effective Biblical Counseling*, 165.

23. Sweeten, *Apples of Gold*, 62.

Selected Bibliography

Ackerman, Robert J. *Children of Alcoholics: A Guidebook for Educators, Therapists, and Parents.* Homes Beach, Florida: Learning Publications, 1983.

Apthorp, Stephen P. *Alcohol and Substance Abuse.* Wilton, CT: Morehouse-Barlow, 1985.

Augsburger, David. *Caring Enough to Confront.* Glendale: Regal, 1980.

Beattie, Melody. *Codependent No More.* New York: Harper & Row, 1988.

Benner, David G., ed. *Psychotherapy in Christian Perspective.* Grand Rapids: Baker, 1987.

Carnes, Patrick. *Out of the Shadows: Understanding Sexual Addiction.* Minneapolis: CompCare, 1985.

Cook, Jerry, Stanley C. Baldwin. *Love, Acceptance and Forgiveness.* Glendale: Regal, 1979.

Crabb, Lawrence J. *Effective Biblical Counseling.* Winona Lake, IN: Brethren Missionary Herald, 1986.

_____. *The Marriage Builder.* Winona Lake, IN: Brethren Missionary Herald, 1986.

Crowley, James F. ed. *Alcohol and Drugs: Working with Adolescents and Schools.* Minneapolis: Community Intervention, 1981.

_____. *Alliance for Change.* Minneapolis: Community Intervention, 1984.

Griffin, Em. *Getting Together: A Guide for Good Groups.* Downers Grove: InterVarsity, 1982.

Hadaway, Kirk C., Stuart A. Wright, Francis M. Dubose. *Home Cell Groups and House Churches.* Nashville: Broadman Press, 1987.

Hart, Archibald D. *Counseling the Depressed.* Dallas: Word, 1987.

Hemfelt, Robert, Frank Minirth, Paul Meier. *Love Is a Choice—Recovery for Codependent Relationships. Nashville*: Thomas Nelson, 1989.

Hestenes, Roberta. *Using the Bible in Groups*. Philadelphia: The Westminister, 1985.

Johnson, Vernon E. *I'll Quit Tomorrow*. San Francisco: Harper & Row, 1980.

Krupnick, Louis B., Elizabeth Krupnick. *Despair to Decision*. Minneapolis: CompCare, 1985.

Kübler-Ross, Elisabeth. *On Death and Dying*. New York: Macmillan Co., 1970.

Malony, H. Newton, Thomas L. Needham, Samuel Southard. *Clergy Malpractice*. Philadelphia: The Westminister, 1986.

May, Gerald G. *Addiction and Grace*. San Francisco: Harper & Row, 1988.

McDowell, Josh, Dick Day. *Why Wait?* San Bernardino: Here's Life, 1987.

Miller, J. Keith. *Sin: Overcoming the Ultimate Deadly Addiction*. San Francisco: Harper & Row, 1987.

Minirth, Frank, Paul Meier, Siegfried Fink, Walter Byrd, Don Hawkins. *Taking Control*. Grand Rapids: Baker, 1988.

O'Gorman, Patricia, Philip Oliver-Diaz. *Breaking the Cycle of Addiction*. Deerfield Beach: Health Communications, 1987.

Parker, Bob. *Small Groups: Workable Wineskins*. Cincinnati: Christian Information Committee, 1988.

Peck, M. Scott. *People of the Lie*. New York: Simon and Schuster, 1983.

Sowder-Capell, Kathy and Others. *Codependency: An Emerging Issue*. Pompano Beach: Health Communications, 1984.

Stanley, Charles F. *Handle with Care*. Wheaton: Victor, 1988.

Sweeten, Gary R. *Apples of Gold I Teacher's Manual*. Cincinnati: Christian Information Committee, 1983.

VanVonderen, Jeffrey. *Good News for the Chemically Dependent*. Nashville: Thomas Nelson, 1985.

Ward, Charles G. ed. *The Billy Graham Christian Worker's Handbook*. Minneapolis: WorldWide, 1984.

Wilson, Sandra. *Counseling Adult Children of Alcoholics*. Edited by Gary R. Collins, Ph.D. Dallas: Word, 1989.